UNLIMITED

JILLIAN MICHAELS
UNLIMITED

A THREE-STEP PLAN
FOR ACHIEVING YOUR DREAMS

THREE RIVERS PRESS
NEW YORK

Published in the United States by Three Rivers Press, an imprint of the
Crown Publishing Group, a division of Random House, Inc., New York.

www.crownpublishing.com

THREE RIVERS PRESS and the Tugboat design are registered trademarks
of Random House, Inc.

Originally published in hardcover in the United States by Crown Archetype,
an imprint of the Crown Publishing Group, a division of Random House, Inc.,
New York, in 2011.

Library of Congress Cataloging-in-Publication Data

Michaels, Jillian.
Unlimited : a three-step plan for achieving your dreams /
by Jillian Michaels.
   p.   cm.
1. Self-realization.   2. Self-actualization (Psychology).
3. Success.   I. Title.
BF637.S4M496 2010
158—dc22   2010050834

ISBN 978-0-307-58831-9
eISBN 978-0-307-58832-6

PRINTED IN THE UNITED STATES OF AMERICA

Book design by Elizabeth Rendfleisch
Cover photograph by Andrew Southam

10 9 8 7 6 5 4 3 2 1

First Paperback Edition

This book is dedicated to the people who have educated, inspired, and mentored me tirelessly with love and care. Suze Orman and K.T. Travis, my second mommies. I look forward to all the "Suze smack-downs" and K.T. home-cooked meals my future holds! Dr. Phil, my fearless protector, I swear I will try to stay out of trouble so you can enjoy your spare time again. And of course Dr. Jo Ann McKarus, my mom, without whom I wouldn't exist physically, spiritually, or psychologically. I love you.

CONTENTS

ACKNOWLEDGMENTS

Special thanks to my brilliant team who work around the clock to help make the world a happier, healthier place:

My business partner, Giancarlo Chersich—without you I am lost.

My exceptional editor and sparring partner, Heather Jackson, and all the badasses at Crown Publishing. I am so blessed to have your literary genius as my guide.

My valiant and talented writing partner, Claudia Herr. I am amazed you have any hair left after tussling with me project after project.

My dedicated and steadfast right hand, Rosie Acosta. I am loath to put your last name on the page lest anyone discover you're the brains behind the operation and steal you away.

My loyal crack team at Empowered Media: Ray, Danny, Autumn, Julie, and Tammy.

My beloved lawyer, David Markman.

My gangster team at CAA—Kevin Huvane, Steve Lafferty, Alan Braun, and Lisa—for never letting me accept Plan B.

Ellen Rakieten, producer extraordinaire, it was meant to be.

Jay McGraw, Andrew Scher, and the Docs, thanks for letting me crash the show and always getting my back.

Mouse, for her endless support and patience.

And last but not least, my crew at Everyday Health who are the power behind my website, JillianMichaels.com.

INTRODUCTION

"The mass of men lead lives of quiet desperation."
—HENRY DAVID THOREAU, *WALDEN* (1854)

God that quote pisses me off.

Why? Because it's true—but it shouldn't be and doesn't have to be.

There is absolutely no reason why you can't live your dreams, no matter what they are; no reason you can't live the life you've always wanted. Look, you have dreams for a reason. Call it your destiny, your karma, your life's mission, whatever you want, but your dreams are what define your place and purpose. When you live in fear of your own desires and ambitions, you lose sight of your true calling and your true self. Life loses meaning, and inertia sets in. You become depressed, unhappy, and start to wonder: *Is this really all there is?*

The answer is NO!

Every human being has the capacity to transform suffering or weakness into peace, power, strength, health, and abundance. **There is no authentic goal you can set for yourself that can't be reached, no dream that can't be realized.** It's just a matter of learning HOW to achieve what you want.

That's what this book is: a how-to for wish fulfillment. Many self-help books tell you what to achieve, but they don't give you particularly useful tools for how to achieve it. They offer a lot of New Age platitudes and sappy self-help mantras:

> *Just love yourself.*
> *See the glass as half full.*
> *Believe it and it will come.*

I mean, really. That's not how it works, and you know it.

A lifetime's worth of struggle is not overturned in a moment of positive thinking. But if you have the right attitude *and* skills, you can and will accomplish anything and everything you want. This book gives you both: attitude and action. By its end you'll have all the tools you need to change your life—no hype, no false promises.

So what are we talking about: Career? Love? Emotional health and physical well-being? Yes, yes, yes, and yes! This book is a manual with only one purpose: to arm you with the strategies you need to achieve anything you desire and become whoever you want to be. *Unlimited* gives you a step-by-step plan that will enable you to begin a purpose-filled, meaningful life according to your truth and on your terms.

I know what you're thinking: *What's Jillian Michaels doing writing a self-help book? She's the fitness guru, right?* The fact that people think of me as a fitness guru is hilarious. I imagine a fitness guru as someone who wears spandex, feels the burn, and loves an endorphin high, then follows it all up with a shot of wheatgrass. That is *so* not me! What I do is not about fitness. Exercise is just one of the tools I use to help people rebuild their lives.

If you referred to an architect as a sketch artist, he would look at you like you were an insane person. Architects help people build homes; sketches are just one tool they use to do it. Well, that's what fitness is to me—a tool I use to help you build a life. It's *never* been just about the sit-up. Even my fitness best seller, *Making the Cut*, is at its roots about striving for excellence in your life, not just at the gym.

So here we are, with a life to build and no exercise routines to suffer through. Don't panic—we won't need them. This is about being healthy in *all* aspects of your life. If getting physically healthy is your focus right now, check out one of my last three books. This book is about everything I do with my contestants behind the scenes that never makes it into the episodes cut for TV (well, maybe some of it on *Losing It*). It's about the quieter but necessary steps for transformation, the nuts and bolts of what I do to be successful in my own life, and the tools I use to help others get there as well. It isn't about calorie counting or ab crunching; it's about self-exploration and discovery.

All you need to begin is courage, conviction, and faith, both in yourself and in me as your guide. Sure, at first the faith-in-yourself part is hard, but that's where I come in. See, I don't just hope you can do this—I *know* you can.

Lean on me while you get stronger. And trust me: you have unlimited potential and the ability to fulfill it. We all do—it's just that some of us know it and some of us don't.

Now, get ready, because it's time to stop being quiet and desperate. Screw surviving—it's time to THRIVE. Unlimited health, wealth, and happiness are just waiting for you to claim them.

I can't promise you it's going to be easy—think about it, nothing worthwhile ever is, is it? Achievement doesn't come without risk and sacrifice. But what I can promise you is that I will cut out the crap and tell you what works. Come with me on this journey, and your life *will* change dramatically, for the better.

So let's dig deep, get our hands dirty, and do this.

STEP ONE
IMAGINE

This is one hell of a journey you're beginning. In fact, it'll probably be the most important, challenging, and rewarding thing you ever do. But as I'm sure you know, every journey, no matter how huge, begins with a single step. So what is that first step in taking control of your life and beginning to live the way you are meant to live? Simple. (Notice I didn't say easy.) Your first step is to let your imagination run wild. To live the life of your dreams, you have to know what those dreams are.

So in Step One, I will teach you how to get a firm grip, mentally and emotionally—and yes, even spiritually—on what it is you want out of life. This is the fun part. This is where you get to kick aside any ideas that may have taken root about your life being set in stone on its current path, or about your not being worthy of a truly great life. The title of this step really says it all—this is where you get to imagine everything you have ever wanted your life to be.

CHAPTER ONE

IDENTIFY YOUR PASSION

(Or, What the Hell Do You Want to Do with Your Life?)

If you've picked up this book, chances are you're looking for a change. You may feel like something is missing from your life, but you don't know what it is. Or you may be stuck in a rut, waking up every morning wondering how you're going to make it through another day.

If this is you, I'm so glad you've come to me, so I can tell you, in as many ways as I know how, that that is not what your life is supposed to be! We were all born with the desire and the right to be happy. But somewhere along the way many of us got trained—by family, friends, religion, society at large, whoever—to believe that the human condition is predominantly one of suffering. And if we're not happy, it's just because "that's the way things are." That is *the greatest lie ever told*.

We're taught to settle, and we're made to feel guilty if we single-mindedly go after something we want. We go on to believe that our desires are selfish. That our self-love is arrogant and pompous. All our joy and innocence are stripped away as we're programmed like androids to live lives of servitude and "responsibility." Too many of us buy into the idea that there are rules to how this life works, and dues that must be paid.

We grow up being told that if we behave and play by the rules, the good life will happen for us in some vaguely defined future. Parents preach this in the home. Teachers preach it in the classroom. Bosses preach it in the workplace. This belief is handed from generation to generation to generation. But for most of us happiness never comes. That's because society is built on the repression of individual desires. In the distant past it would have been impossible to maintain any kind of social order unless people thought they *had* to take on the jobs and responsibilities that the society required. You know what I mean. Someone has to do all the crap jobs that no one wants.

Socialization is the transformation of the human organism into a person who functions in a social system. And the most effective method of socializing people is to make them identify so thoroughly with the social order that they can no longer imagine themselves breaking any of its rules. History has shown us that that's super scary, right? In the past, socialization was enforced through rewards and punishments based on basic human needs for survival. *Step out of line, and we'll kill you. Speak against the government or religion, and we'll take away your livelihood so you can't feed your family anymore.* These are extreme scenarios that, while unfortunately still playing out in many parts of the world, are far from our reality here. Times have changed, and most countries are democracies. So if you want to stop working at some shitty job, or accepting some shitty life, luckily no one is going to come kill you or take all your dough.

You might be thinking, *But if we all upped and started doing whatever we wanted, it would be anarchy!* Not true. Society *would* continue to function—it would just be forced to evolve. Let's take a very basic example. Hypothetically say that all the train conductors in the country decided to quit their jobs and follow their dreams to open their own businesses. The economy would be just fine, and eventually so would the trains. Each of the new businesses would generate jobs and local income, and if we're savvy enough to put a man on the moon, I think we're savvy enough to develop technology to run trains without conductors.

WAKE UP and think about it: society tells us it is okay to want things, but only within reason and at a price. We are allowed to want comfort, but in due time and within limits. A happy marriage with 2.5 kids and a picket fence is cool, but a sprawling estate on the California coastline, being married to the person of your dreams, doing what you love as a career? *Who the hell do you think you are?*

Imagine a college student saying, "I want to be a billionaire by the time I graduate." You and I both know that most people would call that student an upstart and say that was an outrageous, arrogant statement. People would smack that kid down! The attitude, from parents, teachers, and society, would be "Who are you? That's not how life works. You have to pay your dues like the rest of us." And maybe the student would let it affect him or her—or maybe not. Clearly the founders of YouTube—Chad Hurley, Steve Chen, and Jawed Karim—chose not to let anyone smack them down, and they ended up selling their company to Google for a cool $1.65 billion. (And the founders of Facebook, MySpace, and Google wouldn't be smacked down either.)

Let's be clear, I'm not saying money buys happiness, but these successful innovators are not just people with money. They are people who made money doing what they love.

Ask yourself this: how much deprivation, how much self-effacement must you suffer before you act on your desire for meaning and fulfillment, before you thrive in your life instead of barely surviving it?

Now, don't get me wrong. You can't skip the process of learning. You *do* have to go to medical school before you can practice medicine. But there's no rule saying you can't be the best brain surgeon in the entire world upon graduation. The truth is, there are no rules. Period. Anything is possible if you have the knowledge and do the work. In fact, not only is it possible, it's critical!

We are here to cultivate our passion, fulfill our dreams, and take this exquisite experience called life to its apex. The human condition isn't about suffering—it's about achieving and being all that we can be. Sure, suffering is a part of life, but it's not all there is. Its counterpart is joy!

> **"Your joy is your sorrow unmasked. And the selfsame well from which your laughter rises was oftentimes filled with your tears. And how else can it be? The deeper that sorrow carves into your being, the more joy you can contain."**
> **—KAHLIL GIBRAN**

Suffering and joy are connected, and though we will inevitably experience pain, joy is our true destination, and the right of the human spirit.

Unleashing our passion and pursuing the things we want bring us to our truth, allowing us to become whole and to make our dreams into reality (or as some would put it, to "manifest our destiny"). Ultimately, that is what you owe the world. When you are healthier and happier, you are in the best position to give back to your loved ones and to the world at large.

I'm sure some of you are thinking, *I wasn't brought up like this. I was taught to be humble and accept my lot.* Yeah? Well, so was I. Let's be clear: wanting things and feeling worthy of a great life do not mean you think you are more deserving or better than everyone else. We are *all* deserving of happiness. Those of us who throw off society's conventions to attain our goals are showing others that it's possible for them as well. Don't mistake healthy ego strength and prosperity for greed and ostentation.

People may try to shake your resolve, but be strong. Don't cave—lead by example. People can be slow to change, but they'll follow your lead eventually. Even if they don't, do not compromise your happiness because of others' lack of insight. You owe it to yourself and to the wider world to max out your potential.

We could spend a lot of time pondering how we've been

programmed to believe we have to settle for less, and how this fallacy has infiltrated our collective psyche. But seriously, what's the point?

Let's save ourselves some time here, kick the *should*s of life to the curb, and call bullshit on this pernicious piece of dogma. Listen to me very carefully: it's time to start living your life the way God, or (insert whatever greater power you believe in here), intended—HAPPILY.

Got it? Good.

DREAM IT, DO IT

Think about it: there *are* happy people in this world. Some people's dreams really *do* come true; I'm living proof. Real happiness exists for some, so why not you? I love to use Oprah as an example, because her experience speaks louder than any counterarguments you could give me. She was a poor, sexually abused African-American kid, growing up at a time when racism was still a painful reality. Now she's one of the most powerful women in the world. She made it to where she is without a single starting advantage. If she can be that successful, why can't you? Absolutely nothing makes her different from you in any way that makes *her* level of success unattainable by *you*, if you were to decide you wanted it.

I'm not saying you have to be a mogul or an icon to be happy and fulfilled. I'm just saying that when it comes to success—whatever that might mean to you—the sky's the limit. Quite literally, if you can dream it, you can have it—provided you're willing to do the work.

Sadly, although dreaming should come as naturally to us as breathing, many of us have forgotten *how*. We've become terrified to hope, paralyzed by thoughts of failure, ashamed of our desires—for no good reason. By muting our hearts' desires, we lose the ability to listen and guide ourselves toward our true purpose. We end up going about our lives quietly and somewhat comfortably numb, not experiencing the lows but not experiencing the highs either. We're not really living—we're merely existing. That's just plain wrong. And it's the first thing we're going to change together.

As we are sentient human beings, our ability to dream is one of our greatest gifts and freedoms. No one but you can take your dreams away from you. It's sad that so many of us have lost the ability to dream, because it's what allows us to develop our innermost selves to be in tune with the natural harmony and abundance of the universe. Now when I say "natural harmony and abundance of the universe," please don't think I mean life's going to be all rainbows and butterflies from this moment on. In fact, contending with hardship is often how we find our inner strength and our most authentic selves. Many of our greatest awakenings occur in the freefall of life. And please don't take me for a fluffy New Ager—I happen to have a spiritual bent myself, but you don't have to have one, or have discovered yours yet, to get everything there is to get out of this book. I'm also a science girl, as you'll see in Chapter 3, and everything I'm talking about can be looked at from that perspective as well.

We were brought into this world at this time and place for a reason, and our one and only responsibility on this planet is to find out what that reason is, no matter how long it takes. The meaning of life is not some truth that is handed down to you—it's something you create for yourself, by living authentically and by cultivating your passions in any and all circumstances. As Paulo Coelho, one of my favorite authors, said so beautifully in *The Alchemist,* "When you want something, all the universe conspires in helping you to achieve it." The only catch is figuring out what your passion is, what it is that you love to do. You may first have to relearn how to dream so you can identify what you really want out of life.

Some of us know what we want and always have. If this is you, you're way ahead of the game—A+ for you, you get to pass Go, collect your $200, and move on to Chapter 2. Most of us don't have this kind of clarity, though, which is how we end up feeling lost. Often when I talk to people about pursuing their passion, they confide in me, with concern, shame, or panic, that they don't know what they are passionate about. Don't worry, this is a common problem.

A lot of us have shut down the part of ourselves that relates to and nurtures our joy and inherent passion. We've given up hope of enjoying life to the fullest because we're scared of being perceived as selfish or ego driven, or because we're afraid of disappointment. It can be scary to have dreams if you're programmed to think that they won't come true, or that you're somehow a selfish ass if they do.

Others may feel that dreams are just for children, like unicorns or Santa Claus. Grown-ups don't dream—we're practical, we do what's expected of us, and we follow a bunch of rules even though we can't remember who told us to or why. (Yeah, that sounds pretty grown-up to me.) We hide this load of crap inside what I like to call a responsibility sandwich, but really it's glorifying the idea of being a martyr—and just another way of trying to make a miserable life more palatable. Awesome. If this is you, no wonder you're unhappy! You're wildly off base and out of alignment with your higher calling—and that SUCKS.

Living life without a dream, an ultimate goal, is like being on a ship that's lost at sea. Think about it. When you plan a trip, you need to factor a lot into your preparations: which direction you need to go; how far you're going; how much fuel you'll need; how much food you should bring; what clothes you should pack; and on and on. Seeing to all of these details prepares you for your journey and ensures that your trip will be smooth, right? But if you don't have an end goal in mind, then how can you prepare? And as has been said before, failing to plan often means planning to fail.

Why not apply this principle to your life? If you don't have an end in mind, how can you work on getting there? It's a surefire way to get lost.

Some of you are going to tell me that there *is* no destination, that life's in the journey. And while there is truth to that idea, *technically* you're not on a journey if you don't have a destination in mind. Without an end goal, you're just engaged in an exercise of wheel-spinning. Sure, it takes a lot of energy and work, but there's no real movement or progress. For your life to take the course it's supposed to take, you have to get on the road first. Then you have to sit in the driver's seat.

You know that saying "Life is what happens while you're making other plans"? Well, that really is true. But the key to a successful life is that you're making plans, actively pursuing a goal, putting positive and powerful energy into the universe, and staying open to what comes back to you. This is totally different from wandering aimlessly and hoping happiness will just find you. It won't! You have to pursue it, actively and in good faith. (Hey, this is even in our Constitution. You want to mess with the Founding Fathers? I didn't think so.)

Okay, so you get it. It's important to know where you're going, to have a goal. But how do you find out what your goal is? Like I said, most of us have forgotten how to dream for fear of disappointment, judgment, or whatever, so this is where I'm going to give you a little push. Nothing scary. I'll provide just a few simple exercises to help you relearn how to cultivate your talent for dreaming and find exactly what you're meant for. You do it by learning how to find meaning on scales large and small.

When I was a kid, every Easter my mom would stage a massive egg hunt for me in our house. Man, I loved Easter. Halloween, too. Basically any holiday where candy was involved. I would go bananas, running all over the place, turning over every pillow, looking in every potted plant, scavenging through bookshelves, rummaging through drawers. You get the idea—I was *very* enthusiastic. Anyway, I'd always miss some of the eggs, and when I was ready to throw my hands up and quit, my mom would play the hot/cold game with me. You must have played this as a kid. The closer you get to the object of desire, the "warmer" you are; the farther away, the "colder."

Okay, so you're not a kid looking for Easter eggs. But you're a valuable human being looking for your purpose. So in an attempt to revive a childlike zest for life, we're going to play our own little hot/cold game to help you uncover all the things that are important to you and that give your life meaning.

COLD, WARMER, HOT: UNCOVERING YOUR DREAMS, FINDING YOUR TRUTH

At the end of this chapter there is a place where you can fill in your answers to the questions I'll lead you through, and on my website there's also space for you to "journal" your journey. So no matter where you are, you'll have the tools you need at hand to "do this." But read the questions carefully first and really think on them. Work it out for yourself. Along the way I'll throw in some inspiring stories so you can see this stuff in action. (Would I tell you to do something if I didn't know you'd get results?) The questions will have you focus heavily on your professional life, the reason being that our purpose on this planet is to *do* something that makes us happy and allows us to leave a mark. Yes, we'll talk about how to find love and how to get healthy. But this journey starts with what you actually want to *do* to express your unique value to this world. Very few of us know what we want to do with our lives in the larger sense. The idea is to start becoming conscious of and paying attention to what makes you happy (warmer) and what doesn't (colder), so you can build on those things and move toward your true calling.

Throughout the book you will see sections under the heading "Working It Out." Wherever you see this heading, it means you have work to do. So I want you either to grab a journal and keep it handy while you're reading, or sign in to JillianMichaels .com and use the "Working It Out" journal on my website. You can log all the internal work we're doing together, as well as all your goals, dreams, and aspirations. I've also created a number of online assessment quizzes so you can dig even deeper. Look for this icon ✍; it's your cue to log on to JillianMichaels.com/Unlimited to take a quiz and to get your results, and to find other special online tools, charts, and support designed to enhance your journey. This is your space—use it, own it, work it.

TAKE STOCK OF YOUR WORK AND PERSONAL HISTORY

Look deeply into your experiences, and try to identify positives, negatives, and common threads. Maybe you're really good at public speaking, or organizing people, or working with computers. Make a list, and keep working on it over days and weeks; as you do, pay attention to your heart, and listen to the thoughts that emerge in those rare quiet moments. If it doesn't happen overnight, don't worry, and don't push it. Chances are you will see a pattern emerge in your experiences, one that will lead you to discover the innate passions that drive you, fulfill you, and make you happy. Again, at the end of this chapter you'll find a section where you'll be able to work on this, as well as additional questions to nudge you along the right path.

How One Person Found Her Calling

My close friend and personal yoga instructor Heidi Rhoades provides us with a perfect example of how destiny takes its course when you stay open, listen to your heart, and cultivate your passion.

Back in the late '90s, Heidi was a confused teenager (like most of us were as teens) attending college at Penn State. At that point in her life she had no idea what she wanted to do over the course of the next week, let alone the rest of her life. Being smart and practical, Heidi met with a counselor. This counselor suggested she go into marketing. Here was the logic: "If you go into marketing, then you're not tied to anything because you can do marketing in any field." Great plan, right? Just be utterly noncommittal and maybe one day happiness will find you. Oy.

So years later Heidi was a very successful and very unhappy marketing exec in the music industry. She had the right clients, the right office, the right clothes, the right car, and still . . . she was miserable. None of it made sense to her. She had followed all the rules and achieved what she thought was the American dream. But she hadn't achieved the ultimate and seemingly elusive goal of finding true meaning in her life.

She diligently slogged through her days like a good soldier, believing that being able to pay her bills and live comfortably came at a price. The price of happiness. Granted she had friends and loved ones she cherished who brought her joy, but professionally she was sucking it up. Now here's where the story gets interesting.

One day Heidi's company decided that they wanted to start healthy initiatives for their employees. One of which was having a yoga instructor come to the office and teach classes for the company staff every Tuesday and Thursday after work.

Heidi, however, allowed these perks to go unnoticed. Months went by and she didn't even pop her head in, let alone attend a class. This is not because she wasn't athletic. In fact, Heidi had grown up as an athlete. She had done gymnastics, danced, played soccer and softball, was the star of her high school track team, and to illustrate life's irony, in college she was actually an accomplished yogi. Now, however, she was an adult. She had meetings to run and lunches, dinners, and drinks to attend. "What focused professional would have the time to be frivolous and take a yoga class?"

Well, on one Thursday, after a heated phone call with

another industry exec, and having already put sixty hours into her workweek, she suddenly felt as though her heart were going to pound out of her chest. She broke into a sweat, her breathing was constricted; she felt lightheaded, and the room was spinning. She was having a major anxiety attack. Heidi immediately went to the office kitchen to grab a glass of water, and who was there prepping for her class? I bet you already guessed it—the yoga teacher. She sat with Heidi for a while, helped her regain her composure, and ultimately convinced her that yoga would be a great way for her to de-stress and maintain some semblance of calm in her life.

At this point, feeling particularly vulnerable, Heidi was ready to listen. She scooped up the workout clothes that she kept in her car in a gym bag, which had gone unused for well over a week, and took the class that day. Although her flexibility and strength were a bit rusty, she loved it. She felt an inner peace and sense of tranquillity that had been eluding her for years. And thus her love affair with yoga and its ability to heal and transform people was reborn.

To make a semilong story longer, Heidi began taking classes and workshops with top instructors from all over the world. She began teaching her coworkers and friends in her spare time, simply because it brought meaning into her life when she saw them find joy and restoration through yoga practice.

Eventually she reached a crossroads. It became clear to her what her true calling was meant to be. She had always thrived through athleticism as a child, and she had serendipitously rediscovered her passion for it as an adult. Continuing a career in the music business seemed an unbearable and absurd proposition at this point. Once a person steps into the light, living in the dark is an impossibility. And while at first the idea of quitting and trying to break into a new field was scary, she knew her passion lay in practicing and teaching others yoga, and she followed that with certainty.

Today? She's a very happy, very successful yoga teacher living in Los Angeles working with people from all walks of life, from A-list celebrities to women in domestic violence shelters and special-needs kids. By listening to the messages the universe was sending her and following her passion, she made a change and is now doing what she loves and loving what she does. Which is just how the universe wants it!

MAKE A LIST OF YOUR HOBBIES AND INTERESTS

Your true calling may lie hidden in something you *don't* do to pay the rent. Can't wait to get into the garden every spring? Love to cook for family and friends? Do you spend your weekends quilting, knitting, or doing something else crafty? There is no reason you can't turn your favorite pastime into a career. Look at all the amazing entrepreneurs out there who did just that: Martha Stewart started a catering company out of her basement. Her *basement,* people! Coco Chanel started out as a seamstress with no formal training in fashion or design. Walt Disney dropped out of high school at sixteen to animate cartoons.

Oh yeah, and then there's me: a seventeen-year-old kid who fell into fitness training because exercise made me feel strong. Martial arts turned me from fat kid to fit kid, and by my late teens I had become a gym rat. One day at seventeen, I was training for my black belt, screwing around in the gym trying an inverted, gravity-boot body curl-up, when someone asked me if I was a trainer. It was the first time that had ever happened. I paused, thought it out, and said, "Sure, I'll train you." And the rest is history. I know what you're thinking: *But that could never be me.* Why the hell not???

When you honor yourself, when you really tune in to your wants and needs, you can't go wrong, and the rewards are endless.

So look closely at all the things you do for fun—think big, stay open, and don't judge. An extracurricular activity could be your best business bet, bringing passion and direction into your life in ways you never imagined possible.

MAKE A LIST OF YOUR APTITUDES AND PREFERENCES

Are you great with numbers but bad with words? Good at delegating or better at being in the trenches? Are you an introvert or extrovert? When socializing, do you like crowds of friends or one-on-one time? As you make your way toward your dream, be sure to pay attention to your strengths and weaknesses, the things you can and can't deal with, the things that curl your toes in delight or that make you want to stab yourself (or someone else) with a fork. Using myself as an example (again), growing up I always wanted to be a doctor. I wanted to take care of people, make them feel better, heal them, and teach them how to stay healthy. There was just one small problem: I can't stand the sight of blood. I get queasy, weak-kneed—not really traits you associate with a good doctor. But I broadened my horizons and found other ways of fulfilling my purpose. I'm in the health biz, just a different area, where I have the freedom and enormous privilege to help people get well and stay that way, without having to deal with the gore of medicine. Everyone wins. Remember, there are many different ways to skin a cat, as the saying goes. As you find your way, let your natural abilities and disabilities, likes and dislikes, guide you.

PAY ATTENTION TO YOUR VALUES AND ETHICS

You'll be miserable in any endeavor that creates a major internal conflict or ethical dilemma. For example, if you're passionate about animal rights, you're not going to be happy working for a cosmetics company that tests its mascara on bunnies. I mean, duh. A lot of people don't realize that sometimes the lines can get blurred. No amount of money, prestige, or convenience can make up for compromising your core beliefs, so make sure you're pursuing avenues that are in alignment with your moral center.

Personal Values

My mother is probably the most ethical person I know. Truth, honesty, and self-awareness are cornerstone values in her life, and she strives to keep her ego in check. (She tells me she is not always successful, but I don't see it; she also tells me I idealize her.) Posturing, superficiality, and shallow definitions of happiness have no place in her life. Her personal belief is that the key to fulfillment and satisfaction is to live one's life with integrity and meaning.

Back in the day, my mother had a successful and glamorous career in public relations. From the outside it seemed like a perfect fit. She's creative, which helped her come up with unique pitches for her clients. She's a people person, which helped her tame even the toughest Hollywood types. And she's beautiful and dresses well, so she even looked the part. She started out in the entertainment field. But when a certain actor, who shall remain nameless, threw a tantrum because he didn't get the cover of *Newsweek* or *Time* to promote his comic book movie in the midst of an international crisis, she was stunned. She fled to corporate PR, hoping to find a saner environment. What she found was enormous pressure to pitch and spin the media in order to portray one's clients in the most advantageous way, regardless of truth or reality. This high-powered, glamorous career left her feeling miserable and empty.

After doing some serious soul-searching, she decided to go back to school and pursue a career in psychotherapy. She so loved her work that fourteen years after being licensed, she decided to further her professional development by earning a doctorate in psychoanalysis, a goal she is close to achieving. Today she is a successful therapist, living her life happily, authentically, and in harmony with her true calling.

You may have the right skills to do a job well, but if they don't correspond with who you are at your core, you're not going to be happy. Take a long hard look at what you believe, and make sure your actions reflect your spirit.

TRY IT, YOU MIGHT LIKE IT!

Is there anything you've always been curious to try but that has always seemed too "out there" or too far afield from your life? How do you know whether you'll like something if you've never done it?

It is crucial that you stay as open as possible to what your true calling might be. A lot of us rule things out before we have the experience or information to judge them. Of course, that doesn't stop us from judging them. More often than not, when we react to something new, it's negative. It's just the way we're programmed.

I see this all the time on *The Biggest Loser.* On season seven, for example, I decided I was going to teach my team how to surf. (Okay, so I wanted to go surfing. Why shouldn't they come, too?) But I thought I was never going to hear the end of the bloody objections: "We're fat, we can't surf." "I don't like sand getting everywhere." "It'll be cold." "I'm going to look like Orca in my wetsuit." Bitch moan, moan bitch—it went on for *days* leading up to our beach outing. The day came. They got into their suits, onto their boards, and into the water. Then something amazing happened. (I knew it would all along, not to brag or anything.) Every single one of them fell in love with surfing. They got to meet other surfers who came to hang out and help me teach them and give them pointers. They got to see dolphins and seals playing just feet away from them in the ocean. They got a great workout paddling around, and they even caught a few waves. Suddenly I had a pack of surfers on my hands. Now it was "When can we go out again?" "Can I try a different board next time?"

Our lives can get pretty routine, and sometimes what you need most is to shake it up a little, try something new, out of the norm, something that feels out of your comfort zone. Don't be afraid to get a little crazy. You don't know if you'll like something until you try it, so don't cut yourself off, out of ignorance or fear of the unknown, from opportunities that might hold the key to your future.

WORKING IT OUT

I'm pretty discerning about whom I take advice from. But when I think someone has wisdom to offer, I'm ready to listen and evolve, and I try to learn new things every day. So I'm going to quote another writer I love, Dr. Wayne Dyer, who said: "Being in-Spirit is a direction we take, rather than a destination to be reached. Living our life in-Spirit requires us to determine that direction, and we do so by noticing our thoughts and behaviors. . . . Once we begin to observe our thoughts, we realize that there are many times we're going in the opposite direction."*

That, in a nutshell, is what this chapter's thought-exercises are about. Your answers to the questions have to come from your heart, not from your head. Don't write something down because you think you should. This isn't about what anyone else thinks you "should" be. It's about you finding out who you are. The key to finding your meaning is authenticity, so really listen to yourself as you think about all the questions. Remember, you are here for one reason and one reason only: to be you, no matter how long it takes to figure out what that means. That's really your only choice anyway. Everyone else is taken. So that's your job, and the only contribution you need to make to the world.

* Dr. Wayne Dyer, *Inspiration: Your Ultimate Calling* (New York: Hay House, 2006).

WORK HISTORY, EDUCATION, AND VOLUNTEERING

- Do you like the structure and resources of a corporate environment or do you prefer a more casual, intimate setting?
- Do you like the adventure of a start-up or the relative stability of something more established?
- Are you more comfortable with physical labor or sitting at a desk?
- Have you enjoyed giving back to the community in a particular way, like helping out at the Humane Society or delivering meals to the homebound elderly?

HOBBIES AND INTERESTS

- What is your favorite thing in the world to do?
- Did you like drama class in college or some other pursuit that you've since abandoned?
- In your "ideal day," what do you picture yourself doing?

APTITUDES AND PREFERENCES

- Do you like the independence of working alone or the collaboration of working as part of a team?
- Are you good at scientific pursuits or are you more of a creative type?

VALUES AND ETHICS

- What beliefs are you most passionate about? Are you an animal lover, a humanitarian, an earth lover?

TRY IT

- Have you always wanted to try skydiving, hang gliding, or something else crazy? Or have you ever wanted to take a class in business management, or something a little less "crazy"?

CHAPTER TWO

IT'S ALL IN THE DETAILS

After the last chapter's work, you should have a general idea of what your big dreams are. Now we'll fine-tune.

Many people assume that once you have a general direction, you're all set. Not so. When you have a vision for your life in place, you need to break it down into smaller goals, clearly defined milestones that help you measure your progress and stay on track. "Making more money" and "getting married" are fine dreams to have, but they are not goals. It's like the difference between saying you're going northeast and saying you're going to the Empire State Building. One is just a point on the compass, the other a definite location. With the first, you'll have no clear idea when you've found it. With the second, you'll know when you've arrived.

If you are not crystal clear about what you want to accomplish, you're likely doomed to spend your life working for the goals of those who are; you will wander aimlessly or build a life that's not right for you. You may make some money but hate the job in which you make it. You may get married, but it might not be a healthy marriage replete with love and respect. If you aren't specific about your goals, your life won't resemble anything you consciously set out to create. And ultimately you will be left with the sinking feeling that maybe you took a wrong turn somewhere along the way, asking yourself, *How on earth did I get here?*

I'm going to refer back to my *Biggest Loser* contestants again. Every day I spend hours, and I do mean *hours,* beating the crap out of them physically and chipping away at them emotionally. I do this daily wrecking-ball routine because to rebuild something from its foundation, you have to break it down first. But to be successful, the contestants have to know it's worth it. Otherwise it becomes torture and abuse—nothing more than a pointless punishment. And it's a punishment that seems to know no end, until they are eliminated from the *Biggest Loser* ranch, thanking God it's finally over. So where is the building part of the exercise? In their intention, in what they are going after in the process.

They must bring to their experiences a clear and deliberate intention to make their dreams a reality. I first help them attach to a dream, as we discussed in Chapter 1, so they understand that all the pain they are enduring has a purpose and a meaning. Then I help them fine-tune it with detail and clarity, so they can move beyond pain to health and happiness. So when we go into the gym and I'm administering the beatings, they visualize their bodies getting leaner, stronger, and healthier, and they envision all the details of what being thinner and in better shape will mean for them. They think about how sprinting on the treadmill will translate to sprinting after their young children at play. How lifting weights in the gym will allow them to carry their fiancées across the thresholds of their homes. You get the idea.

Again, whatever the dream is, as you work toward achieving it, you must keep it in your sights. Nietzsche said in his book *Twilight of the Idols,* "If we have our own *why* of life, we shall get along with almost any *how.*" Most folks don't love broccoli or the StairMaster, but they are worth putting up with, even embracing, whether your goal is to wear skinny jeans or to one day meet your grandchildren's grandchildren—or both.

You may have seen me ask the contestants why they want to be on the show—to fine-tune their intentions. Without fail, they *always* hit me back with the same answer: "Because I want to be healthy." They'll look up at me, smiling, so sure they've given me exactly the answer I want to hear, and that now I'll lay off them, go easy on them, or pick on someone else. Yeah, right.

That answer is lukewarm, to put it generously. In the geographical analogy, it's like saying, "I'm heading northeast." If you asked someone where they were going on vacation and they answered you that way, you wouldn't have any idea where they were actually going. Well, it's the same with saying you want to "be healthy." What does being healthy *mean* for *you*? What does it look like physically, personally, and professionally?

Does it mean living to see your grandchildren graduate from college? Does it mean running a marathon? Does it mean wearing skinny jeans or having sex with the lights on? Does it mean being debt-free and owning your home? Does it mean being happily in love and in a stable, supportive relationship? Does it mean all of the above?

Let's look at the fine lines and details that create your dream. What does your dream really look like? Let's crystallize that vision so you can start to bring intention to even your smallest actions, so that everything you do is a step toward realizing that dream.

Here's a strange but true fact about us complicated humans: our brains can't actually distinguish all that clearly between real events and imagined ones. So by using creative visualization, you can harness the power of the mind to define your purpose. Using your imagination, you can create a memory bank of positive experiences that will motivate you and improve your self-image. In turn, these visions will help you believe in your potential to make your dreams a reality. There is a right way to do this. Let's go through it step by step.

WORKING IT OUT: MASTERING THE DREAM

CREATE A REALISTIC VISION

In creative visualization, you don't get to defy the laws of nature. Don't imagine yourself flying, becoming invisible, or magically making your mother-in-law disappear. Nothing ridiculous, okay? I know this sounds silly, but a lot of times by creating goals that are impossible to achieve, we set ourselves up for failure. Your vision has to apply your dream to your life realistically. Certain things about yourself aren't going to change. For example, if you're five foot three (like yours truly) and love basketball, being drafted into the pros is not a realistic vision. You're never gonna be able to dunk like LeBron. You can become a great player, though, and join a local amateur league, an international team, maybe even coach. Get the idea?

BE SPECIFIC

The more detail you can add to your vision of success, the better. For example, if you are visualizing yourself in a new job, remember to picture things like the commute, your new wardrobe, the way you'll look in the clothes, the kinds of people you'll be meeting, the work hours, and the potential sacrifice in time for family or hobbies. Even picture the kind of workspace you'd like—the light, the sounds, and so on. Use your current life as a template, and think of how your days will change moment by moment. The more details you throw into your vision of yourself as a success, the more vibrant and alive it will become in your mind, and the easier it will be to work toward it.

FEEL IT

You need to associate emotions with the things you are imagining for yourself. Attaching feelings to your visions will make them more real to you. As you visualize your dream job, picture what it will feel like to come home every evening knowing you have worked all day at something fulfilling and meaningful. Picture the excitement you will feel if you achieve your goal. Really enjoy this part of your visualization—let your emotions sweep you up.

When I was a kid, my dad had a vintage muscle car. As a kid I thought this car was the coolest thing in the entire world. I saw it as the ultimate symbol of success. Once I had one of my very own, I would know I'd made it. But my fantasy didn't stop there. For years I imagined ripping around Malibu in that car. I'd feel the exhilaration of roaring through the canyons. I'd revel in the sense of freedom that would flood over me as I drove down the coast, breathing in the ocean air. Well, that vision became a reality. In 2008 I bought a '67 Camaro convertible, and I have literally lived every single one of those imaginary scenes again and again. Whenever I'm feeling stressed out or overwhelmed, I go for a drive in that car, and I'm instantly happy, just as I was in my imagination all those years ago. It's superficial, maybe, but it's my dream, so back off and start working on your own.

By connecting to your visualization emotionally, you can approach your dream as though it already exists. Instead of marinating in sorrow at not having what you want, switch it up and indulge in the feelings that come with experiencing exactly what you want. You get what you give, so try at all times to come from a place of feeling life's abundance. Send this kind of positivity out into the cosmos, and you *will* get positive things back. (See Chapter 3 for a whole lot more on that.)

SENSE IT

Engage your physiology, and you can bring your body in on the visualization as well. I want you to feel the physical sensations in the vision. If you're visualizing a swish at the free throw line, feel the powerful jumping movement explode through your legs and then the descent of your body lowering back down to the ground. If you're visualizing being fifty pounds thinner, imagine what it will be like to fit into a great dress and walk around feeling slim and healthy. If it's your dream to teach kids how to ride horses, imagine how it will feel to be outside all day. Feel your vision as if you're already there and it is actually happening to you. By connecting emotion to physiology, you are completely engaging yourself. It may sound silly, but top athletes use this particular technique a lot, and studies have shown that Olympians with the most gold medals incorporate visualization into their regular practice. Attaching physical sensations to your mental musings makes them all the more familiar and real.

GET EXCITED ABOUT THE PROCESS

You may be thrilled at your vision of success, but can you generate the same positive feelings when it comes to doing the work to achieve your goal? If you visualize yourself winning the Tour de France, can you see yourself sticking with the strenuous practice schedule needed to get there? The strict dietary guidelines? Do you see yourself being okay with spending that much of your time on it? Will you be able to find the process enjoyable and empowering? You must envision yourself being happy doing the work to achieve your goal—because there *is* going to be work.

Think about what you're actually going to have to *do* to get where you want to be, and then feel the joy that doing these things will bring you. If you can't get excited about the work, then your ultimate vision may be out of alignment with your essential being. You don't have to love every second of every step of your journey. But overall you have to be able to see yourself doing the work, going through the process, and finding happiness within it.

CREATE A VISION BOARD

Vision boards are kind of a thing right now—even Oprah's doing them. I have to tell you, they're kind of fun, a little like being in an arts and crafts class at summer camp. The idea is very simple, although you can get as creative and elaborate as you want. Get a corkboard and assemble images and pictures of your goal. Put anything and everything you want on there. Seriously. Houses, cars, awards, luxury travel, six-pack abs. Go to town, be shameless. See a picture of something else you want? Slap it on there! I'm always adding to mine. I'm on my third corkboard.

This exercise is key in that it urges you both to have fun and to learn more about your dream. It's sort of a visual equivalent to writing your goal down (which we'll get to in Chapter 10). It helps you guide your mind toward positive thoughts of success, solidify your agenda, and form that all-important emotional connection to the things you want. Keep your vision board where you will see it as often as possible. Put one in your office. Create one as a screen saver. The more exposure you have to your goal, the more it will become a reality in your subconscious mind.

The bottom line: visualization is a powerful tool used by world-class achievers across every field. It doesn't matter what college you went to or how privileged you are. Those who truly know what they want outperform everyone else by miles.

I want you to practice visualization whenever possible: in the morning when you first wake up, to bring direction to your day; throughout the course of your day, to bring awareness to your immediate actions, no matter how small or inconsequential they may seem; and before you go to sleep, to reflect on your day and refocus for the next. Your imagination can create fear and limitation, but it can also break right through it. Start using it to your advantage to create a new, positive reality.

CHAPTER THREE

SAY A LITTLE PRAYER

(That's Right, I Said *Prayer!*)

Okay, get ready, because this is the most controversial part of the book. If we're talking about realizing your dreams, there is something we MUST cover, and that's the power of *prayer*. If that word gives you the jitters or hives, or just makes you a tad uncomfy, you can call it *meditation, manifesting your reality, wishing on a star*—call it whatever you need to get through this chapter. They all basically mean the same thing. They're all about the act of concentrating on a hope and tapping into a source of energy bigger than yourself to turn that hope into a reality.

People who write self-help books tend to pussyfoot around this issue, not wanting to use religious terminology for fear of turning readers off or upsetting the masses. As you probably know, I'm not one to pussyfoot, so before we go on, I need you to jettison any stigma that you may or may not have attached to words like *God/universe, spiritual, prayer,* and so on, because what I'm about to share with you is absolutely critical to your success. And I'm going to be using those words. Whether you're a believer or not—and I use the word *believer* as loosely as possible—there is no denying the power of our minds. Whether we're talking about praying, meditating, or simply focusing on a goal, scientific

SAY A LITTLE PRAYER **29**

proof shows that what we think and believe have a *huge* effect on our reality.

Proof Positive: Scientific Studies of Mind and Spirituality

The past fifteen years have seen great and growing interest in researching the power and efficacy of prayers, meditation, and mindfulness. Many of these studies raise more questions than they answer, since the unquantifiable nature of spiritual phenomena (such as prayer, compassion, and meditation) presents a challenge to traditional scientific methodology. But the more studies that are done, the more scientists are realizing that valuable insight can be gained from the power of the unseen over the seen, of what we traditionally think of as the unreal over the real.

One of the most fascinating and controversial topics in this field is the power of praying on behalf of other people. The past ten years especially have seen an explosion in the number of studies done in this area—more than six thousand! David R. Hodge, of the College of Human Services at Arizona State University, conducted a comprehensive analysis of a number of these studies, and in 2007 he concluded that, with all variables taken into account, sick people who were being prayed for tended to have better recovery rates than sick people who were not being prayed for. In other words, prayer *has been proven* to be effective in creating very real positive outcomes.*

Okay, next up: the power of meditation. This one is

* "Does God Answer Prayer? Researcher Says 'Yes'," *Science Daily* (March 15, 2007), http://www.sciencedaily.com/releases/2007/03/070314195638.htm.

tough because meditation is even more unquantifiable than prayer. But slowly scientists are opening their minds to the idea that intense meditative training can have all sorts of powerful positive effects on your physical and emotional well-being, and consequently your life as a whole. The studies are ongoing, but so far the research indicates that focused meditation can at the very least have profound effects on our brain chemistry, enabling us to increase positive emotions such as compassion and forgiveness simply by harnessing our minds.[*]

A truly weird but amazing study on the power of the mind comes from Japan. Dr. Masaru Emoto, author of *The Hidden Messages in Water,* wanted to see if anything happened to water at a fundamental physical level, when various mental and verbal forces "acted" on it. He exposed water to blessings, anger, love, hate, and a whole range of human emotions and expressions. After exposing each container of water to the different forces, he froze the water and photographed the crystals. The crystals from the water that had been exposed to love and blessings were consistently and noticeably more beautiful than those from the water exposed to negativity. He has also shown that the same effect can work across vast distances.[†]

None of the above prove the existence of a god out there or the absolute quantifiable power of this stuff. But it does prove beyond a doubt that what goes on in our heads is strongly connected to what goes on in the world around us.

---

[*] David Biello, "Meditate on This: You Can Learn to Be More Compassionate," *Scientific American* (March 26, 2008), http://www.scientificamerican.com/article.cfm?id=meditate-on-this-you-can-learn-to-be-more-compassionate.
[†] From the film *What the Bleep Do We Know!?* (www.whatthebleep.com).

I'm not asking you to abandon your beliefs—don't worry, this chapter doesn't come with a side of Kool-Aid. But you *need* to be able to expand upon them, question them, and open yourself up a little to the things I'm going to tell you and to the concepts we'll be exploring. I'm asking you to keep enough of an open mind that you can take this next step with me. Revered philosopher and spiritual teacher Krishnamurti once said, "Truth is a thing that is living, and to a living thing there is no path—it is only to dead things that there can be a path. Truth being pathless, to discover it you must be adventurous, ready for danger." Often we are frightened and search for a path to reality and truth as a means of security via an organization, a belief, or a guru. But to do that is like being a blind man clinging to a wall, ultimately closing you off to all possibilities, including the very thing you were searching for in the first place.

Upending yourself in this way may disorient you a bit in the moment, but if you are strong enough to endure this loss of bearings, the end result will yield limitless hope and potential. And what have you got to lose, anyway? If your life were perfect, would you be reading this book right now? So relax, don't be uptight, and go with it.

Let's start with something fun: we'll take a stab at defining the common essence of religion, subatomic physics, psychology, biology, and neuroscience. (What the hell, someone's gotta do it, right?) Okay, so I may not be able to unite spirituality and science definitively once and for all—I'm ambitious, but not delusional—but I do know there's a link between them. Ultimately, of course, I can only speak to what I have studied and to how this holistic, integrated approach to understanding the world has changed my life and helps me to change others' lives every day.

I'm probably one of the most spiritual people you'll ever meet. Yes, I curse a lot, and I'm tough as nails, but I am also spiritual. And although I am close to "God," science is at the root of my spirituality. Let me explain.

I believe that everything in the universe is made up of energy and information, including you, your emotions, and your belief systems. Your body, your being, is no different in its makeup from the body of the universe, of God, or (insert whatever vernacular you prefer). The universe is clearly purposeful, with an intelligence supporting its creation and continuing evolution, and we are pieces of this intelligence by virtue of having emerged from it. The energy that you are focusing on this page right now is exactly the same as the energy that created and sustains our world. At an even more literal level, according to astrophysics, the atoms in our bodies once belonged to stars far away in time and space. In every way, you are the universe, and the universe is you.

Am I getting too New Age kooky for you? Just chill out and bear with me. No one ever died from an open mind. Your thoughts and intentions, the things you focus on and hold in your mind, trigger a transmission of energy and information out into the world. By choosing to change the energy and information within your own body and mind, you can literally change the energy and information you send to the world around you. In doing so, you can eventually cause things to change in your favor.

Your journey to a purposeful and inspired life begins when you acknowledge the primordial creative power within you—the godliness—and then harness that power to achieve the results you desire.

GETTING WHAT YOU WANT: (SOME OF) THE SCIENCE

If you're getting a little twitchy at the mention of God, we can actually throw that word out of the equation altogether if you need to. The fact is, faith and spirituality have positive effects on us physically and emotionally via our biochemistry alone—no god about it.

Mind-body medicine has become so widely accepted, it's difficult to remember when it was considered one step up from mumbo-jumbo witch-doctoring. It's even got a fancy name: psychoneuroimmunology or PNI. It's the study of how your thoughts (that's the *psycho* part) affect the chemicals in your brain (*neuro*) and the hormones that fight disease (*immunology*).

But the mind-body connection goes far beyond disease—it relates just as much to our mood, our overall wellness, our outlook on life, and ultimately, whether we get what we want out of that life. What it boils down to is this: nonphysical things, like our thoughts, emotions, and moods, affect our bodies on a cellular level. Anger, fear, joy, love—each has very specific effects on our physiology. Being happy and fulfilled is healthier than being frustrated and miserable. So by sending out wishful vibes (read: dreams), you are actually preconditioning your body to experience the results you desire through your hormones and body chemistry. If you have trouble with the idea of a higher power, or supporting intelligence, you can say that prayer, or sending your hopes out into the physical world around you, is useful because of its benefits to your biochemistry.

We can take this mind-body connection still further and apply it to psychology. You may think your thoughts are just your thoughts, that they're inside your head and that's where they end. Dead wrong.

The way you think, even in the deepest part of your subconscious, affects your behavior in ways you can't see. Your behavior in turn shapes your reality, again in ways you often aren't aware of. Being as simplistic as possible, you could say that positive thinking makes us act in positive ways, setting in motion a chain reaction that turns a situation's outcome our way. We will get into this in more detail later in this chapter, but for now let's just think about this idea for a minute. If there's something you want, and you believe you can achieve it, you will automatically conduct yourself more assertively and confidently. You'll *feel* successful, even if you haven't achieved it yet. You might speak up in a meeting at work, get noticed by your boss, and get that promotion. You might strike up a conversation with that guy or girl at the dinner party, and he or she might ask you out. Get the idea?

The things you think, in general and especially about yourself, form the basis of your every action, large and small. Feeling strong and confident frees you to take the powerful actions needed to get powerful results.

Now, let's go a little further out on that limb—in fact, as far as we can go: geek out with me as we delve into quantum mechanics. (Don't get scared, this will be simple.) Quantum mechanics deals with the nature of matter and energy at the atomic and subatomic levels. Remember at the beginning of this chapter I said we're all made up of the exact same energy as everything else in the universe? What I was getting at was the belief among quantum physicists that everything is made up of strings of energy. Atoms, once considered solid matter, are now known to be composed of pulsating energetic vibrations.

Since everything in the universe is made up of atoms, that makes us all one. Not in a "Kumbaya," let's-all-hold-hands sense but in a literal subatomic-composition sense. We each emit our own unique energy, what quantum folks call vibrational frequency. It is a specific wavelength of energy that changes according to our will and consciousness.

Because all of us and everything in the entire universe are connected by energy and information, when you hurt, it hurts. *Literally.* When you are happy, the vibration of the universe rises a little. Okay, maybe very very little—you're not going to have parades thrown in your honor around the world if you get that raise; after all you're one person, and the universe is, well, *the universe.* But that doesn't make it any less important for every single one of us to find the joy and meaning in our lives. This goes back to my point about the absurdity of thinking it is selfish to follow your dreams or to want to create happiness for yourself.

When you look at it from a quantum physics perspective, you actually owe it to yourself, to everyone you know, and yes, to the universe, to find your purpose in life, so that you can find your optimum "frequency," and contribute to the harmony of the big picture.

If quantum mechanics is too much for you to take, think about this. We can't see atoms, right? But we all know the power harnessed within them. Look at the atom bomb! Well, we're made up of millions of those little suckers. That's a hell of a lot of energy. You just have to choose to harness that energy to work for you, rather than against you.

No matter how you come at it, the undeniable truth is that your energy and consciousness determine the outcomes you will experience, and ultimately the life you build. What seems like magic to some is actually the workings of the energetic world. What some wonder at as mystery, others see as the expression of scientific patterns. Either way, you are a force, and by taking control of the cosmic power we all contain, you are tapping into a source of infinite abundance, accessing all the insight and power you need to achieve everything you want. (Yes, I'm still going to talk like this even after the physics. Get over it, this stuff works!)

GETTING WHAT YOU WANT: THE TECHNIQUE

So how do you harness all this power for your benefit?

By broadcasting a message that is in alignment with your greatest hopes and desires.

Even in your sleep you're sending and receiving energy. In our daily lives television, radio, phone, and satellite signals pelt us from every direction; if we have the right receiver apparatus, we are able to interpret them. Well, you're kind of like one of those satellites, picking up signals from others and projecting ones of your own into the world around you. Whether you realize it or not, your life is a direct result of your personal energy field. The good news is that if you don't like what's coming in, you are free to change the energy and information you're sending out.

It's all well and good to talk about broadcasting your desires, but you have to do it in a very specific way. You attract what you feel, not what you "ask for," so it's imperative that you come from a place of abundance and peace rather than deprivation or fear. It works something like this: the energy we emit is electromagnetic (*magnetic* being the key part) and driven by our emotions, which affect our biochemistry and our atomic makeup and thus play a huge part in what we communicate to the world.

Think of it like throwing a boomerang (if anyone actually knows how to do that): whatever you think and feel comes back to you. And thus the word *karma*. So if you're going to broadcast your desires, you have to come from a place of *have* instead of *have not*.

Whether you want true love, a sports car, or a successful new career, you can't ask for anything if you're focused on your lack of it, because that's what you will invite into your life: lack. Instead, think about what it would feel like to already *have* what you want. Imagine you have already found your soul mate, bought that Porsche, or started that home business. Use those powers of visualization we talked about in Chapter 2, *really* feel the happiness and contentment that you imagine your success will bring you. This way you send a message of affluence and comfort out into the world and invite the same to come back to you. These powerful prayers from positive emotions will establish the first connection between your dreams and your reality.

Let me give you a couple of examples of how this can translate to real life. Say you want a promotion. Don't be jealous of your successful coworkers, because you will be sending the subconscious message that you are less than they are. Instead, focus on yourself and how you can advance in your career by using your passion and drive to get better at your job.

If you want to meet your true love, don't focus on wanting someone to take away your loneliness or make you feel less unloved. Instead think about everything you have to offer the right person, and imagine the beautiful, productive relationship you will have, which is what you will project and attract.

If you want to be healthy, don't think to yourself, *I don't want to get sick*, because that message focuses on sickness. Instead think of feeling strong and joyful and vibrant; your appreciation will put positive, deserving energy out into the world.

If you can desire it, the universe *can* produce it. Think about it: all this great stuff is happening out there. People are falling in love, making money, and enjoying great health and deep fulfill-ment. So these things exist—and it's time they existed for you. I know this chapter has gotten a little "out there" for some of you, but I'm trying to help you recognize the flow of abundance in the universe so that you can tap in to it, allow it to rush into your life. Oprah allows it. Derek Jeter allows it. Mick Jagger allows it. I allow it. Name anyone you admire—he or she allows it. Are you going to tap in to it, too?

Now, here I must slap you back to reality a little. I cannot be emphatic enough on the following point: you MUST bring action to your aspirations and intentions. Prayer and meditation and everything I've talked about are powerful, effective, *passive* methods, but if you don't do the work, if you don't take precise, methodical action to make your dreams a reality, they most likely will never materialize.

This step doesn't stand alone.

You can't just think promotion, you have to kick ass at your job. You can't just think love, you have to put yourself out there and meet people. You can't just think healthy, you have to take care of yourself, eat healthfully, have fun, and exercise.

Everything I'm telling you in this chapter, the prayer, the meditating, the broadcasting, all of it is necessary to make *room* for cosmic intervention, but when that intervention comes, you'd better be ready. There's no such thing as luck, so kiss that idea goodbye. Life is about preparation meeting opportunity. When your destiny comes calling, you'd better have taken the proper actions so you can rise to meet it, or you could blow it.

This action part is the key to why so many of the self-help/law-of-attraction books already out on the shelves are ultimately not very helpful and even potentially harmful. Like a diet book that tells you that you don't have to count calories, they prey on your apathy and indirectly encourage lethargy and laziness. They'll talk about the power of positive thinking and tell you that if you just wish it, it will come, but they leave out the part about putting in the effort. In effect, they tell you it is okay to be a passive bystander watching your life rather than living it full throttle.

This type of entitlement talk is dangerous. Having the right to happiness means having the right to earn it, not having it given to you without effort and action on your part. When people start believing that progress is inevitable and life is easy, they may lose the courage and the determination needed in the face of adversity. This doesn't mean that our natural state isn't contentment and happiness; it just means that success in life is a proactive formula. Often we have to fight for what we believe in and persevere. Remember the old saying "God helps those who help themselves"? Make it your mantra.

Books that promise success without action sell because their messages are easy for people to swallow, but they don't work. The formula is incomplete. You'll notice that this book has three parts. That's because this book is *not* BS. This is just the first step; it's important, but without the other two, it's useless. Sort of like an engine with no gasoline. Dig?

Even if you are a manifesting machine, visualizing your goals and bringing action to your intentions, sometimes in life things don't turn out the way you want. In life there are such things as paradoxes, when outcomes contradict our expectations. But if our intentions are good, our actions will be, too, and they *will* have a positive result, even if it's not the one we expected or thought we wanted.

Let's say that I want McDonald's to go out of business, and I visualize their stores closing down and being replaced by their opposite, healthy mom-and-pop restaurants. I take as much action as possible to make it happen. I spread the word about McDonald's use of unhealthy ingredients, I picket outside their restaurants, and so on. Here's the catch: simultaneously, McDonald's CEO Jim Skinner is dreaming the exact opposite. He is visualizing billions of people walking through those Golden Arches to buy his burgers and fries. He is starting initiatives like the dollar menu to bring people flocking to his franchises in droves.

Bottom line: one of us will NOT get exactly what we want. But remember that on a subatomic level, we are all one and all connected. So when our intentions are in alignment with the greater good, positive things *will* happen.

Maybe you're thinking, *What's the point? If I want something and someone else doesn't, what are the chances I'm going to be the one to get my way?* The reality is that when you put that intention and action into the world, it *has* to come back to you. It might not look *exactly* how you'd planned. I might not shut down McDonald's, but my efforts to do so might inspire McDonald's to offer healthier menu options and alert their billions of customers to pay attention to the foods they are eating and get healthier. I might even end up opening my own chain of health food stores to help to change the world, and I might find happiness in that endeavor, despite the fact that McDonald's is still a profitable company. And down the road, McDonald's might do something with their profits that helps to cure a disease like cancer. I doubt it, but hey, you never know.

There is just no telling *what* might come of your actions if you take them with deliberate and positive intention, and that's where you have to trust yourself and the things you do. They will pay off, but possibly in ways you didn't expect, and you must keep your eyes open so that you can recognize life's blessings.

Think on this: no positive thought or hope goes unrewarded. So stay present and focused in each moment and bring your A game to EVERY situation, no matter how unrelated it may seem to your goal. Intend the best and take positive action at every turn, whenever possible. Transformation isn't a future event, it's a present activity, and the closest you can come to predicting what your future holds is to start creating it now.

Before we get to Step Two, I'm going to leave you with a personal anecdote.

In my midtwenties I wasted several years of my life at a talent agency, pursuing a career as a Hollywood agent. I toiled away miserably, thinking that this career was what I wanted. Well, life took its course, and I was fired. I was devastated—this wasn't part of my plan. What was I gonna do? How would I make money? Ultimately that circumstance forced me back into personal training, which is where my true fate lay. At first I fought it, but I needed the money, so I took a job as a physical therapy aid and personal trainer at a sports medicine facility. Almost immediately I remembered the strength and joy I'd gotten out of being healthy and helping others do the same. I began to understand that my true calling was in the world of health and wellness.

By twenty-eight, I was happy again and back to doing what I loved, but I was still somewhat frustrated that I had wasted four years of my life in a career that wasn't right for me. I believe that everything happens for a reason, but for the life of me I couldn't see the reason for those lost years. I had started out as a personal trainer, and did it from the ages of seventeen to twenty-three. Why the detour? I put that perplexity aside and stayed focused on the positive; I had made a change and was following my heart *now*. And soon I realized that my real passion was in getting people healthy in ALL aspects of their lives. And not being one to do things halfway, I wanted an international platform from which to get my message out. So I began to meditate and pray on it. In the years to come, that platform would manifest, and in the process, I would realize the incredible value of my time there.

It turned out that *because* of the relationships I had formed while working in showbiz, I started to get a lot of celebrities and industry execs as clients. When I went on to open my own sports medicine facility, it took off largely because of connections I'd made during the four years I'd "wasted" as an agent. Here's the cherry on top: during my time at the agency, another agent became a friend and was now working out at my gym. He had heard about *The Biggest Loser* and persuaded NBC to hire me for the job. Had I not worked with this guy for those four years, and had I not been able to build a high-profile clientele, I never would have gotten the chance to be on *Biggest Loser*. All those seeds of effort paid off—just not in a form I had expected.

You see, it's the stuff from Step One that brought opportunity to my door. I had figured out where my passion was, I'd visualized it clearly, and I'd prayed and meditated to create a new reality for myself, focusing my mind intensely on my dream. All of that ripened the circumstances that led to my getting the job with NBC. But once that chance came, rather than sitting back in contentment at landing the job, I worked my ass off to rise to the occasion. Had I not done so, I would likely have bombed at the audition and never heard from them again. Or I would have gotten the job but sucked at it, and my career would have been over before it began. Ultimately, the combination of will, fate, and hard work brings it all together.

I know I'm on TV, not the average profession, and mine is not the average life, but yours doesn't have to be either. I promise, the same principles apply to you, whoever you are and whatever your situation.

I'm not here to try to change your fundamental beliefs about God or religion, but chances are your beliefs, whatever they are, can happily coexist with what I've laid out here. Nor am I out to forever end the science-versus-religion debate—if Einstein couldn't comprehend God, chances are I'm not going to be able to answer those profound questions either.

What I do know, though, is that prayer, visualization, manifestation, and meditation *work*. I have seen it firsthand in my own life and in the lives of my teachers and students, people in all kinds of professions and from all types of backgrounds. (And if my word's not good enough, I even threw in a little scientific proof for you.)

Your mind is *powerful,* but you have to choose to make that power work for you. It can imprison you or set you free, depending on how you think and what you believe. Which brings us to the Step Two of the system: learning to believe in yourself.

STEP TWO
BELIEVE

Now that you've done the work of figuring out what you want, it's time to start the internal work of assessment and reconfiguration to believe in your ability to achieve it. I can sit here all day teaching you how to connect with your passion, how to bring your dreams out of the dark. I can talk until I'm hoarse about your incredible power to be the architect of your own reality. I can even give you a step-by-step plan to help you bring action to your life-changing intentions—that's coming in Step Three. There's only one catch.

If you don't believe in yourself, in your power to change, and in your deservingness, if you don't REALLY believe you can achieve your dream, you won't. It's that simple. We all have the ability to turn ourselves around and start living our dreams; the only reason you're not living yours right now is that your life experience so far has stripped away your belief in your unlimited potential.

So in this step I'm going to teach you how

to build that belief back up. I will teach you how to reboot your thought processes so you can stop getting in your own way and start letting your power work for you. You'll learn to channel and move through fear, redefine your self-image in the light of acceptance and love, bolster your positive self-esteem, and develop healthy ego strength. Basically, I'm going to make you unstoppable. Up for it? I know you are.

It's a multistep process; it won't happen overnight, and it involves some hard questions and even harder answers. It's going to take courage on your part. You've got to be ready to take some risks, to get out of your comfort zone; you've even got to be prepared to fail, because you will fail—we all do it, and it's a valuable part of the process, as I will explain. I know it's scary to think about change, and the possibility of putting yourself out there and failing. It's common to fear exploring what's uncertain and unknown. But here's the thing: until you are ready to confront these fears and fight through them, nothing's going to change. Remember, what you think and what you believe drives everything you do—or don't do. So let's get your head in the game and out of your way.

CHAPTER FOUR

TIME FOR YOUR WAKE-UP CALL

Hundreds upon thousands of self-help books have been sold based on the myth that change is easy. Think great things about yourself as you're nodding off one night, and in the morning you'll be a new person, the kind who sees the glass half full. Sure, on rare occasions people can "just change," but for the most part that's bullshit. Change is not that easy. We're all carrying around years of emotional baggage, deeply entrenched sets of behavior and defense mechanisms that repeat and repeat as we go about our lives, often seriously sabotaging us. And in many cases we don't even know it. To change our lives, we first have to change our behavior, and to do *that*, we first have to wake up to it. This step is all about identifying the self-destructive things we do every day and getting to the root of the negativity behind them so we can break out and move forward.

You're probably thinking, *Great, here comes the psychobabble.* Calm down. A lot of people scoff at the idea of psychotherapy. Maybe they like the stiff-upper-lip approach to life. Maybe they think psychotherapy is just for psychos. Nothing could be more foolish. Therapy, much like this chapter, is nothing more than a tool for self-discovery, a means to unravel your self-defeating habits and attitudes so you can transform them into behaviors that enable you to live better. Period.

If you're still not convinced, watch what you say, because I've been in therapy since I was five. My mother started me at such a young age because I was really angry at my dad, and it was coming out in the form of night terrors. Therapy literally changed my life, and I've been in it pretty much ever since. Because of my years on the couch, I've gotten to know my dark side, and I've learned how to keep it in check. At this point my self-destructive behaviors are like old enemies that I've done battle with again and again—I know all the angles, all the moves I need to dodge them and prevent them from fucking up my life. "Know your enemy," goes the saying; after years of help and self-exploration, I know my inner enemies, the triggers that make them rear their ugly heads, and the weapons I have at my disposal to sap them of their power.

Understanding how *you* think about yourself and why you react to life the way you do will allow you to change any behavior, knock out any mental obstacle, and create any reality you desire.

Many of us struggle with this type of self-exploration because we interpret our negative behaviors as flaws. This takes a huge swipe at our ego and might leave us feeling empty or worthless: like we are wrong or bad in some way. So we stay in denial and don't work on these negative behaviors. The irony is that *all* people have flaws and destructive patterns, which they play out to varying degrees. What should make you any different? This is part of the human condition, and the ability to acknowledge these shortcomings is the first step toward recovery. To move forward, you must see your shortcomings as opportunities for growth—which is exactly what they are.

Let me give you an example using a former contestant of mine. He was a great guy, but I could see he had a chip on his shoulder the size of Texas. He needed to feel positively acknowledged by everyone around him at all times; otherwise he would go on the attack, suspecting that this person hated him or that person was ignoring him. Really the people he was projecting all this negativity onto were just going about their own lives. But he did it with everyone: other contestants in the house, me, even the show's producers. This behavior pattern was effectively negating the opportunity he was being given on the show, because he was alienating the people around him who were there to help. But because he was unaware of his own behavior, he couldn't stop. And as a result, he was living his life in victim mode and sabotaging his chances of success.

Well, if you know me at all, you know that I was *not* about to let this ride. I needed to show him how and why he was pushing everyone away, so he could eliminate this destructive pattern and improve not just his *Biggest Loser* experience but all aspects of his life. So I set him up one day when we were all at the gym. I worked him and worked him and beat his ass relentlessly for hours, and no matter how well he did, I acted dissatisfied, knowing that denying him the pat on the back he expected would push his buttons in the worst way. Sure enough, not long into the session he lost it, getting angry and upset at me. So I asked him, "Why do you need my validation? Why aren't you able to be proud of what you are doing without my acknowledging it? After all, aren't you here for yourself? This isn't about pleasing me—this is about learning to exercise, learning to eat right, and losing weight. Who cares whether a 'good job' or a 'you make me so proud' comes out of my mouth? My opinion won't affect your ultimate goal of weight loss or health either way."

He got so mad at me, he actually stormed off set, before the workout session was over. That was only going to mean less of a result for *him* come weigh-in, and that would affect his ultimate success.

He had to make a choice. He could ignore the pushy trainer chick, refuse to personalize her mood, and get on with the workout; or he could take everything personally, get really upset, and run away from all of it, leaving anger and drama in his wake. But because he was so in the grip of his unconscious behaviors, sleepwalking through his own life, he wasn't aware of these options, or how his own choices were hurting him in the long run. He didn't see that he had the choice to stay on track with his workout and get closer to his weight-loss goals; he reacted impulsively without understanding the nature of those impulses. He had done that in similar situations all his life, without realizing how much he had been hurting himself the whole time.

Of course I ran him down straightaway to talk to him. Ultimately, I was able to help him understand what he was doing, again and again, in all aspects of his life, and why. It turned out that his dad wasn't around much during his childhood and wasn't all that affectionate when he was. He gave his son no praise or adoration, no hugs of fatherly pride. Naturally this was painful, as it would be for any young man idealizing his dad. And it left him with an intrinsic lack of self-worth, a hole he was constantly looking to other people to fill. His dad forgot his soccer games, missed his graduation, and so on, and he interpreted that to mean he wasn't a good enough son for his father to be engaged and interested. These issues were about his father's shortcomings, not his, but he wasn't capable then of realizing that. He had replicated that dynamic in all areas of his own life, projecting his relationship with his father onto all his present relationships in an unconscious attempt to win approval and get validation. But because he was looking in all the wrong places, he continued to find only frustration and inertia.

Once I helped him wake up to his behavior, he was able to get out in front of it. By recognizing that he was on autopilot, hard-wired to react to his history rather than to his present, he was able to take charge of his daily interactions and prevent these triggers from disrupting his life. He was able to see that whatever he felt in the gym toward me had nothing to do with me, someone he'd known for three weeks, and everything to do with his striving for his father's attention and approval. The situation was a workout session with a tough trainer, nothing more, nothing less. By uncoupling his past from his present, he was able to build up his self-esteem enough to grieve over not having a more supportive dad, move on from it, and arrive at a place where his approval of himself was enough.

BREAKING BAD: SHEDDING LIGHT ON REPETITION COMPULSION

Are you seeing how this syndrome works? If you aren't aware of your issues, you're destined to repeat the same unhealthy behaviors and patterns again and again as you struggle, unconsciously, to make old hurts right. And all the while you're sabotaging the hell out of your life. Therapists call it repetition compulsion. We are unconsciously compelled to fix old wounds. But if you want to see it at work in your own life, it's the reason you always date the same asshole guy, or the reason you continue to attract the same nonsupportive friends, basically the reason you always seem to have the same drama, the same problems.

Often people think that their problems arise out of a lack of intelligence, attractiveness, humor, and so on. "If only I were prettier, smarter," we think, then these bad things wouldn't happen to me. The guy would have stayed. My old boss wouldn't have fired me.

But as you will realize as you go through this process, your problems arise not from your lack of positive attributes but from your lack of awareness of your actions. You're not paying attention to *why* you attracted a guy who can't commit. You're not understanding *why* you have problems with authority, and so you rebel at work.

I have seen people rationalize their issues and problems by blaming circumstances or "bad luck." This is utter crap and total denial. Luck is a lie. Luck, as someone said, is preparation meeting opportunity, and unluckiness is often due to lack of preparation. We create our own reality, and then we have the nerve to ask "why me?" It's true that bad stuff happens to good people, and we'll get into that a little later, but at some point we have to stop living and reacting to life unconsciously and take back our power. We have to stop acting in ways that repeat painful patterns and feelings from the past.

Now, the reason our negative behaviors are unconscious is because they are painful, so we suppress them. But you can't trick the psyche. Things that you don't work on and work out get played out . . . again and again.

No one is particularly keen to look back at his or her life and dig up dirt. It can bring up feelings of anger, sadness, betrayal—often with family members who are still in your life, like your parents. They were your primary role models, after all. They played a hugely significant role in shaping who you are.

No one particularly likes to be angry with their parents. It sucks. It makes us feel separated from them, which brings up primal feelings of abandonment. It makes us feel alone, guilty, angry, and confused. So instead of examining the past carefully, we often say things like "My childhood was great" or "My parents were perfect." We are in denial about the parts of our childhood that were hurtful because we love our parents and don't want to blame them or be angry with them.

Stirring up the past can also make us feel guilty and ungrateful for all the amazing things our parents did do for us. So many people paint life in black-and-white terms: "My childhood was perfect" or "My father was a total asshole." You see, if someone is perfect, then we have nothing to be angry about and nothing to be hurt about. We go into denial, but we end up playing out our unrecognized and unresolved issues with others. On the other hand, if something or someone is all bad, then losing them or being angry at them isn't as painful, because there is nothing good about them to grieve losing. With this attitude, victimization can set in. "Poor me. Things were so bad for me. I've had such bad luck."

I played this black-and-white game for years with my dad. He was a total jerk. There was nothing good about him. I was a victim of having a bad father. Poor me and good riddance to him. But finally the consequences of my attitude, and the behavior it created in me, became too heavy a load to bear. That forced me to wake up, deal with my feelings, and change my outlook. Only when I integrated the good and bad parts of my dad in my heart and head was I able to mourn the loss of him as a father, forgive him for his shortcomings, and stop playing out the harmful dynamic in areas of my life where it was wreaking havoc (like at work with my male bosses, which I will get into a bit more in Chapter 5).

I bet you're thinking, *If this stuff is so painful, why do I want to unearth it? And if I chose to repress it, how would I uncover it?* Okay, one question at a time. If you don't look back into your past and figure out what makes you tick, you won't be able to control how you tick. In other words, you won't be able to control the direction your life takes. Like a watch where the minute hand goes counterclockwise, you will live in a way that takes you backward instead of forward.

I am not saying you should live in the past, but I am insisting you learn from it. If you haven't done so until now, it's time to start. Otherwise you will probably continue to carry this baggage around until the benefits you get from denial are outweighed by the bad consequences it's causing in your life. If you're not ready, stop reading, 'cause if you won't do the work, the rest is pointless. Just know that this book will be waiting to help you out when you are ready.

If you do want to get "real" but don't know how, then start with these exercises. Take a look at your life: long, close, and hard. By getting wise to what your issues and negative patterns are, you can stop them from holding you back. And I don't want to hear "But I don't know what my issues are" or "I have no idea why I do that to myself." That's a cop-out. You have to be brave and look beneath the surface of your life. You TOTALLY know what your issues are, even if you have been trying to suppress them. We can all find our hot buttons and deepest hurts if we look closely enough. Up until now, you may not have wanted to deal with them. But if you want to reclaim your power and your life, you must defeat these patterns.

I want you to answer a series of questions. They're designed to shed light on your destructive patterns and their origins so you can free yourself once and for all. These questions are hard, and the answers might be even harder. If your immediate reaction is "I don't know," you're on to something, and you need to push yourself further. Take your time. Sit with the questions and meditate on them. Ask family and friends for their input, but make sure the answers are all you. This is about searching your soul for the tools to rebuild your self-worth on a new, solid foundation.

If you answer them honestly, these four questions will tell you everything you need to know about how you undermine yourself and why. You date the jerk because he reminds you of your dad and you always wished your dad loved you more. You have problems with authority because your parents were stifling and arbitrarily strict, so now you keep pissing off your bosses and getting fired. You binge compulsively because as a child your parents pushed you toward perfection, made issues of your weight, and weighed you weekly, so now you eat to rebel and show them who's in control. And on and on. Don't be afraid to dig deep. You have to—if you want to lay a strong foundation and build on solid ground.

WORKING IT OUT

What self-destructive behaviors in your life do you want to change? (These are the things you do that you know you shouldn't and yet feel compelled to do anyway.)

EXAMPLES:
Do you drink too much?
Eat too much?
Gamble or shop compulsively?
Cheat on your spouse?
Neglect your emotional and physical needs?

Work too much?

Do you get angry a lot and rage at people?

Do you seek the approval of others to feel worthy?

Do you yell at your kids?

Do you push the people who love you away?

What harmful dynamics, behaviors, and scenarios do you see repeating in your life? (These are the things that you perceive as happening to you, even though in truth you are creating them.)

EXAMPLES:

Do you keep dating assholes who abandon you or mistreat you?

Do people around you always let you down?

Do you get picked on or poked fun at?

Do you keep getting fired from jobs?

Do you continually surround yourself with people who aren't supportive?

Do you feel like no one listens to you?

After you have established the patterns and dynamics that you need to work on, then you need to figure out their origin. You can do this by gauging how these things make you feel, and then attempting to figure out when you first felt this way in your life.

How do you feel when you are engaging in self-destructive behaviors:

Angry?

Sad?

Alone?

Scared?

Helpless?

Worthless?

Neglected?

Disrespected?

Stupid?

Unattractive?

Unlovable?

All of the above??

What other times in your life have you felt this way? And how far back in your life can you trace this pattern?

For example, in the case of that former contestant, he was upset that I was ignoring him at the gym. That made him feel "less than" and neglected. By exploring other times in his life when he had felt like that and tracing how far back it went, we finally got to the root of the problem: in his early childhood his father never spent time with him. He never went to his baseball games, his school plays, and so on. By finding the roots of your feelings, you can begin to understand and resolve them so they don't continue sabotaging your life.

Dig deep into your emotional memory—go back as far as you can. It's going to be painful, but that's how you'll know it's working. Be brave, and know that the only way to go from here is up. Although it's scary to feel these feelings, there are ways to heal them and move forward.

You might uncover shortcomings in your loved ones and explore the ways they let you down. But that doesn't mean they are bad people whom you have to villainize. It simply means they are human, like you and me. Recognizing the way their issues affected you allows you to stop internalizing their stuff and to forgive—both them and yourself. That is where true freedom lies. And that's what we'll discuss in the next chapter.

CHAPTER FIVE

FORGIVE AND ACCEPT RESPONSIBILITY

Once you have acknowledged the issues from your past that are messing up your present, the next step—and it's a crucial one—is to work on forgiving the people who originated them. Most self-destructive behaviors are rooted in childhood trauma, although we can be knocked on our asses as adults, too.

Sometimes crappy things happen to us, and we don't have the knowhow or the resources to prevent them. Sometimes we really *are* victims. The mistake is to internalize the situation and make it our fault: *I wasn't good enough, smart enough,* whatever *enough, to make this person love me, to make that person stop hurting me, to make that person stop hurting themselves.* Sound familiar? And in many cases issues of self-loathing continue to haunt us in our adulthood, manifesting in the repetition compulsion we talked about in Chapter 4.

Fortunately, as you evolve through this self-exploration, you will be able to change these patterns by recognizing them and refusing to let them repeat in perpetuity. Instead you will take responsibility for your life *now* and make different, conscious choices that propel you in positive directions. You *can* free yourself from the shackles of self-loathing, grow from your past hardships, and progress. But nothing can happen until you learn to forgive.

You MUST find a way to forgive the people who have wronged you. You may be thinking, *Sure, this all sounds very enlightened.* But you're pissed, and you're holding on to that anger because whatever asshole hurt or betrayed you doesn't deserve forgiveness. Maybe you think forgiveness means condoning their behavior. Maybe you think your anger at the offender is their punishment, especially if no other punishment is forthcoming; forgiving the person would mean letting them get away with it. You may go so far as to seek retribution—"an eye for an eye" can certainly seem viscerally satisfying. But if you aren't able to actually harm the other person, harboring anger at them can feel like the next best option. Holding a grudge can give you a strange historical sense of justice.

Here's the thing, though: forgiving the asshole isn't for their well-being, it's for yours. If you can't forgive the things that have been done to you—as a kid, as an adult, whenever—then you won't be able to move on with your life. Forgiving doesn't mean forgetting. Nor does it have to mean letting the person back into your life to hurt you again. It simply means healing the hurt that's been done to you and continuing to pursue a prosperous, meaning-filled life.

The psychological, spiritual landscape of forgiveness is tough to navigate, but it's a journey that yields powerful, permanent results. It will enable you to stop taking on other people's issues and stop allowing their shortcomings to define who you are. You will understand that what happened to you wasn't because of *your* limitations but because of the other person's. For this reason, forgiveness comes when you are truly able to gain understanding and empathy for the person who hurt you.

Additionally, learning to let go will free you from the negativity that festers when you hold on to grudges and wounds from the past. Here's a great analogy: soft tissue inflammation is helpful only in the first few days after an injury occurs. After that, if it's allowed to become chronic, it often causes even more damage than the original injury. In the same way, anger is an emotional defense mechanism designed to mitigate pain after a tragedy. It confers a sense of purpose and a motivation, and if there is one thing devastated people need, it is motivation. But anger is insidious, and if it's allowed to boil without being processed and released, it can cause far more harm than the initial offense. Studies have shown that holding on to a grudge can result in depression, insomnia, fatigue, and even high blood pressure. Being angry, fighting with people, hating people, or otherwise feeling wronged drains our energy both physically and emotionally. When we can't let go of anger, we are destined to relive the pains over and over again, allowing the hurts to wreak havoc on our lives. Holding on to a grudge can damage or strain your relationships, distract you personally and professionally from work and family, and inhibit your ability to open up to new things and new people. It basically robs you of experiencing the beauty of life as it unfolds.

GOT A GRUDGE?

When you open yourself up and embrace forgiveness, you release yourself from victimhood. You then can find psychological healing from past wounds, and your life can take on new, positive meaning. If you put old hurts in a context that helps you grow, rather than holds you back, you become unstoppable.

I've touched on this a little already, and if you have read any of my previous books, you already know it, but as a kid I had a *lot* of anger toward my dad. It took me years to forgive him; hell, it took me years to figure out I even needed to. Until I was in my early thirties, I figured he was a total bastard who deserved the anger and hostility I felt for him, end of story. I used my hatred of him to propel me toward success. I was going to become wealthier and more powerful than he was. I would show him. I would have the last word. But this anger was messing me up in many other areas of my life, and ironically it sabotaged the very thing I had set out to achieve—professional success.

My anger really hurt me in my career. For years, I simply couldn't tolerate a man telling me what to do, which proved to be kind of a problem. At work, I was replaying the dynamic with my father by fighting with my male bosses—constantly. Anytime I felt I was being treated unfairly or in a domineering manner, I acted out. It's not okay to be treated poorly, but there are ways to handle things so that they turn out in your favor. I wasn't following that rational course of action, and being a "charged" person in general, I pretty much told them all where to stick it. I got fired from two jobs because of it, and I'm convinced it's the reason I wasn't able to reach a deal with the producers at *Biggest Loser* for the third season.

So one day I was at my therapy session feeling particularly aggravated about the drama in my professional life, feeling sick and tired of constantly hitting the same wall. My shrink tried to tell me that until I could work through my issues with my father and forgive him, the pattern of self-sabotage that had me in its grip would continue. Naturally, because I was also playing out my father dynamic with my shrink, I argued with him. I told him he was crazy, that my father had nothing to do with my work, and anyway, how on earth was I supposed to forgive someone who had done so many awful things to my siblings and me? The things he told me, after I calmed down, literally changed my life.

He explained to me that the key to forgiveness lies in understanding that those old offenses that my father committed were *not* intended against me personally. Whatever was done to you wasn't done because you deserved it, or because you were inadequate, but because the other person had limitations. My contestant's dad was distant, not because of anything the contestant had or hadn't done—not because of anything he was or wasn't—but because his dad had grown up with distant parents himself and never really learned how to give or receive affection. He did the best he could with the tools *his* life experience had given him.

The same goes for my dad. He grew up in an environment that

didn't equip him with the tools to help himself, let alone anyone else. Because of the way his parents raised him, he grew up feeling impotent and hating the side of him that was vulnerable and sensitive. As a result, when he had kids, he projected these insecurities onto us. "This is textbook stuff, all over the pages of psychoanalytic literature. The traumas of our parents that don't get owned and worked out by them get unconsciously passed on to us, their children," says Dr. Jo Ann McKarus, aka my mom.

It was worse for my brother, because he was a boy, and so my dad more closely identified with him. He was constantly berating him, telling him he would never amount to anything, that he was Peter Pan and would never grow up to become a man. The toll it has taken on my brother's self-worth is devastating. But slowly I'm helping him understand that the things our dad did to him weren't really about him at all—they were reflections of how our dad felt about himself.

We're all mirrors that way, projecting and seeing the things we don't like in ourselves onto other people, then blaming them or attacking them for it. If you don't like feeling needy, you will particularly hate neediness in other people because it triggers *your* feelings of vulnerability.

Now you might think, *I am not needy, and that's why I dislike it in others. I never cry. I'm John F'ing Wayne. I take care of myself and so should everyone else.* But if you pay attention, you will see that what you defend against so vehemently is the issue you are struggling with personally. You are so afraid of your own feelings of neediness that you bury them, repress them, and silence them—and then they creep out as projections onto other people. If you weren't uncomfortable with feelings of neediness, you wouldn't care when they express themselves in other people.

As I hope you realize, the pattern isn't about being needy only. It's about any issue that triggers your insecurity and that you defend against. It's because you identify with a feeling on some level, and seeing it in other people triggers your negative reaction. This rule applies to everyone! I guarantee it. And the only way you can stop the cycle is to become aware of your issues so you don't project them onto other people.

Conversely, understanding that the same pattern applies to the people who have hurt you can bring peace. Whatever happened to you was really about their issues, insecurities, life experiences, or lack thereof, not your shortcomings or deficiencies. If you don't come to terms with your issues, then you are doomed to repeat them. As my mom says, the issues get handed down from generation to generation.

My father was the youngest of three sons. He claims to have been nonexistent in his family, feeling that his parents negated and neglected him. They thought he was a "throwaway," he told me, and they focused all their attention on their older sons and their daughter, the baby of the family. My dad was determined to prove his parents wrong and ultimately became a very rich man. His inner feelings of insecurity and worthlessness, however, never went away, because he never worked on them. Then when my brother was born, my father projected all those unresolved issues onto him. If my brother doesn't come to terms with these feelings and resolve them within himself, he will most likely repeat this pattern with his son, and so on and so on.

It's up to you to break the cycle, for your sake and that of your loved ones.

In some cases, we have to come to terms with the fact that we may be more evolved than our parents. I know, it feels slightly unnatural—they're supposed to be the adults, they're supposed to have all the answers, know all the pitfalls, be beyond all the mistakes. But most often they aren't. Think of it like this. Imagine we are all computer operating systems. Sometimes your parents are Windows 95, and their parents were Commodore 64, but you're OS X. And your kids will likely be something even newer, even better, something nanotechnological. Every generation builds upon the knowledge of the last, so it's actually natural for us to end up more evolved than our parents, as painful as it might be to realize it.

There are, of course, exceptions—my mom is one of them. But

a lot of people I know end up as the adults in their relationships with their parents; although this scenario can be tough to take, once you accept it, it can also bring healing.

Most of our issues stem from childhood, but if you are holding on to feelings of being wronged by something that happened more recently, you must open your heart and chart the territory that needs to be covered for forgiveness to occur at a transformational level. When you are truly able to gain an understanding of the person or people who wronged you, then you will stop internalizing their demons and letting their issues destroy your self-esteem and self-worth. Know that a life filled with compassion is a life filled with peace and power, and that will benefit both your physical and your physiological health.

So this all sounds very Zen, right? *Understand, forgive, be compassionate, blah blah* . . . But how? Where to start? Forgiving can be so difficult, especially if the hurtful events you endured were ongoing and traumatic. For this reason, forgiveness will probably not come overnight. It will take time and patience.

COMMIT TO HEALING

Begin the process by making a commitment to heal; that is key. You do it by recognizing how pain and anger are sabotaging your happiness. Do your emotions keep you from being open with your loved ones? Do they drain you of valuable energy you need to focus at work? Do they create havoc for your physical health? Do they distract you from being productive?

Now stop for a moment and think about all the benefits that would come from forgiveness. Imagine how it would free you energetically and emotionally to pursue your dreams. Imagine how your relationships would improve. Imagine how your performance would be elevated at work. And so on.

Next, move on to understanding: not yourself this time, but the people who have wronged you.

Whether it's a parent, a significant other, a nasty professor, a jerk boss, or whoever, start by trying to comprehend who they are. Then investigate and inquire as to why they are that way. For example, my dad was angry, bitter, and critical. When I looked back into his past, and examined the dynamic he had with his own parents, I was able to see where these patterns came from.

A contestant of mine was struggling with critical, judgmental parents. For years she believed that she was a "curse" and a disappointment to her family. When we took the time to look back at her parents' lives and their childhoods, she was able to recognize that her parents came up in a very traditional, strict Chinese household. Her parents had never experienced much warmth or physical affection when they were growing up, so they had no point of reference or inclination of how to be affectionate and loving with their kids. By leaving China to come to the States, they had angered and disappointed their parents (my contestant's grandparents). Her parents felt guilty for not living up to expectations. Then when they had children of their own, they projected those feelings of disappointment onto my sweet contestant; they would constantly berate her for not being "good enough," because inside they didn't feel good enough themselves.

WORKING IT OUT

WRITE IT DOWN

Your first exercise is to write down all the attributes that upset you about the person you are trying to forgive. It could be greed, selfishness, cruelty—you name it. Fire away.

KNOW YOUR HISTORY

Next, begin looking into this person's background. Examine how, where, when, and why these qualities might have developed in them. The greatest sociopaths of our time, from Hitler to Saddam, had horrific childhoods that molded them into the monsters they became. I'm not suggesting the person who hurt you is a genocidal maniac; I'm simply saying that behavior, good or bad, extreme or subtle, has an origin. You can argue nature-versus-nurture all day long, but the bottom line is that a person's dormant ability to do harm will most often stay dormant unless catalyzing life events trigger it. So get your detective cap on, and research the background of your "offender."

But suppose you don't have access to background information on this person. Let's say it's a boss, a teacher, or a new beau, and you don't think they would be open to a line of questioning (joking—sort of), and short of hiring a private investigator, you probably won't know much about why they are the way they are. In this situation, your best bet is to look at the present state of their lives and relationships to see if there is a behavior pattern of poor treatment of others besides you.

For example, a friend of mine was dating this guy who was austere and shut down. She was convinced that if she could be pretty enough, smart enough, and funny enough, she could open him up and make him warm and considerate. We didn't know anything about his childhood, so we could look at only who he was today. We analyzed his professional relationships and his other personal relationships. We realized that he was austere and shut down with *everyone* in his life, not just my friend. He had a young son from a previous marriage who was struggling to connect with him. He was not close to his mother and often spoke of her negatively, in a belittling manner. While he was razor sharp in his profession and terribly successful, the line of work he had chosen required one to be "nonemotional" and fastidious. By analyzing his emotional dynamic in multiple areas of his life, my friend realized that his lack of emotion had nothing to do with her and everything to do with him. He was cold with everyone. Knowing that it wasn't her shortcomings that made him distant gave my friend peace of mind.

It's your turn.

Take a look at the present circumstance of the person who hurt your feelings. Do they hurt others in the same way? Is the crappy teacher crappy with other students? Other female students? Other male students? Has the cold boyfriend been cold with other women? Is the nasty boss an ass to other employees? Is there a pattern in their upsetting behavior? Again, the point is to understand the other person and their issues so you don't internalize them and make them your own. (Chapter 6 is about understanding WHY you allowed yourself to fall into this pattern with an abusive person to begin with and how to change it so it doesn't keep happening in your future.)

DON'T TAKE IT PERSONALLY

Now that you understand the person who hurt you, and hopefully why they hurt you, you can cast off their issues and not take them on as your own. This is a huge step forward.

From understanding you must start to build compassion, as only through compassion can you find forgiveness. The literal meaning of *compassion* is concern and empathy for the sufferings or misfortunes of others. So that is what you are going to do.

I want you to imagine yourself as the person who hurt you. See yourself walking in their shoes, living their life, feeling their feelings. This will allow you to recognize that the person who harmed you is more than just the person who harmed you. They are a full-fledged human being with feelings of their own, and their actions that harmed you came from their own confusion, hurt, and powerlessness.

This exercise allows you to feel sadness for their misfortunes and to see your offender not as evil but as misguided and lost. With this empathy, you're more inclined to find forgiveness and stop feeling angry and resentful.

FORGIVING THE UNFORGIVABLE

It is hard and painful to learn to forgive, but the only way out of the fire is through it; no matter what was done to you, no matter how terrible, you need to do this work to reclaim your power and your life.

There are varying degrees of forgiveness. Forgiving your dad for not showing up at your soccer games is a whole different animal from forgiving a rapist or a child molester. I know. I'm not saying that I would be able to forgive a rapist, but I will put a question to you: what other option have you got?

You can let yourself become consumed with anger and desire for revenge and eventually become a monster. You can internalize those feelings and become a permanent victim of life. Or you can let go, learn from the experience, and move on, wiser and stronger, with empathy and compassion that will improve your life and touch the hearts of many others. The hard truth remains the same: the only way to move forward is through forgiveness.

The wisdom you'll gain from understanding and forgiving brings new responsibility—the responsibility to acknowledge the poor choices you have made and to choose differently. Choose *life*. Which leads us, conveniently, to our next topic: taking responsibility.

WHO'S THE BOSS?
BEING ACCOUNTABLE

Okay, so you have achieved awareness of the issues that lead you to sabotage yourself in the same repetitive, self-destructive ways. You've identified the roots of these issues and cast off the shackles of self-loathing through understanding and forgiveness. Now it's time to take the final empowering step: evaluating the choices you've made in response to your hardships and asking yourself how they've brought about your current status. Stop blaming anyone or anything for your situation or your problems. When you blame others, you are essentially saying that you are powerless over your own life, which, I'm sorry, is bullshit. You are not a victim of life but a participant in it, and you have to accept full responsibility for your life—the good, the bad, and yes, the ugly—in order to regain control.

Responsibility isn't about blame. There's a big difference between blaming yourself and taking responsibility for your choices, your mistakes, and your present reality. Blame is useless and serves only as a way for you to beat yourself up and wallow in negative feelings. Taking responsibility is about empowerment, acknowledging your capability to change things, and moving on from your current situation to something better.

You may be thinking, *But life really has dealt me a bad hand. It's really not my fault that my life sucks.* Just hold on a second. I'm not saying taking responsibility means controlling *all* the things life throws at you—none of us can do that. And there *are* times when we are victimized. Allowing yourself to accept that reality frees you to release any guilt or shame you might be carrying for tragedies and hardships that befell you in the past.

There comes a time in adulthood, however, when you need to take responsibility for how you allow these tragedies to affect you and for how they form you. You can control your *reactions* to life's less-than-perfect moments to affect an outcome that is favorable to you. This goes for situations, circumstances, people, and things.

Something horrible may have happened to you, but you *always* have a choice in how you respond to it. You have the "Why does bad stuff always happen to me? I'm never going to find happiness" option, and the "This sucks but I'm going to learn and evolve from it, examine what role I played in it, and ultimately it will help me become the person I'm supposed to be" option. Guess which one you're going to choose from now on?

Once you become conscious of and take responsibility for how your choices have led you to where you are right now, you can bring a new consciousness to the choices you make going forward. You can choose life, love, and happiness over anger, pain, and sadness. Just as important, you can choose power, focus, and success over helplessness, self-obstruction, and failure. It's up to you whether you let that bad relationship keep you single forever. It's up to you whether to let someone's criticism damage your self-esteem and keep you from piping up with an idea you believe in. It's up to you whether you sit home and worry about being out of work, or whether you take proactive steps to find a new job, or even a new career path, and change your situation. I could go on and on, but you get the idea.

What Choice Did She Have?

Shay is a girl I had the amazing good fortune to work with recently. She grew up on the streets, literally. Her mother was a heroin addict who shot up in front of her all the time. She would lock Shay in a closet while she turned tricks to support her habit. Sooner or later Shay landed in the foster care system and was in and out of one home after another, completely powerless over where she ended up or who took care of her. By the time I met her, in her late twenties, she weighed 476 pounds. Her past had crushed her to the point that she was literally committing slow suicide by eating herself into an early grave.

Now, there is no question here—Shay was a victim. Growing up, she was subjected to just about the worst that any child can experience. Her sick mother exposed her to horrible dangers and couldn't give her the basic love and care that every child deserves and needs. She was the victim of an archaic and bureaucratic foster care system. As a kid, she had no power to control or change her situation. She was *definitely* a victim of circumstances, and her life was pure hell.

But even someone like Shay, who is haunted by a childhood full of pain and fear, now, as an adult, has to recognize her role in getting to where she is now. She has to accept that it was *her choice* to use food to abuse herself the way she was abused as a child. Are her actions understandable? Hell, yes. But can we change them through awareness, forgiveness, and self-empowerment? HELL, YES.

See, the flip side of realizing that you've made bad choices is understanding your power to make *good* choices. By taking responsibility for letting herself reach 476 pounds, Shay has been able to get herself down to 250 pounds. She finally understands that she has the power now. She has the choice to become a permanent victim of her horrendous childhood, living out those patterns of abuse and neglect until she kills herself, or to open her heart to the process of grieving, move through all that pain, and gain strength from forgiving those old wounds. She can move on and build her life on her own terms.

No one could possibly leave a past like that totally behind; it's just not that simple. But by taking responsibility for her current situation, Shay is able to see she has the choice to build something positive now, even on such a painful foundation. She has lost more than 200 pounds and is healthy, living happily in California with her husband and thriving at working with children, a job she loves.

THE PERFECT STORM

For a friend of mine, a lack of awareness, forgiveness, or responsibility created a perfect storm of detrimental outcomes that eventually forced him into bankruptcy.

I ran into this friend recently and asked him how he was doing. He told me he'd had a hard year. He was financially wiped out. He'd gotten a DUI. His dog needed an enormously expensive surgery. His car had been repossessed. All these financial hardships had destroyed his credit, and he had had to declare bankruptcy. Now he couldn't get a loan for a new car, and he was having trouble renting an apartment. Even worse, he was on the rocks—*again*—with his girlfriend. My friend was feeling very sorry for himself, but let's look at how he alone was responsible for his situation.

First off, the DUI: he shouldn't have been drinking and driving! Had he not made that bad choice, he would not have had to spend thousands of dollars in legal fees and court costs. That said, it certainly could have been worse—he could have killed himself or an innocent person. As for his dog's surgery, there is such a thing as pet insurance, and it's cheap! Maybe $150 a year. Had he been responsible and planned ahead by buying the insurance, the dog's surgery would have been covered. The car that was repossessed was way out of his price range, but he had decided to buy it anyway instead of doing his homework and buying a car he could afford. As a result, his income took a big hit. And last, the girlfriend situation was avoidable. This was a girl he had been on and off with for months. He was playing out the same abusive dynamic that he had had with his mother. Had he chosen to do the deeper work on himself, he probably wouldn't have returned to an unhealthy relationship that always left him in the lurch—especially when he was going through a tough time in other areas of his life.

You may think I'm being unduly harsh: *Jillian, where's your compassion?* But is it compassionate to hide the truth? Is it good to foster a friend's self-destructive behaviors? I don't think so.

But let's get back to you. Are you beginning to see the patterns that are holding you back? Nine times out of ten we unconsciously create a reality we don't really want, then blame our problems on "bad luck."

Bullshit.

We are powerful beings who create bad situations in an unconscious attempt to teach ourselves something.

Taking It to the Streets

Here's another example for you, and this one's personal. As I am writing this book, I am homeless, and it is creating a massive amount of stress in my life. A while back I decided to redo my house. I began construction, thinking the work would take only three or so months to complete. I took a three-month lease on a temporary place where we could stay, figuring we would be happily back home by the time it expired. While we were in the makeshift quarters, I decided to rescue a couple of dogs from the animal shelter—bringing my total dog population to four— thinking we would all have a smooth transition from leased home to fully finished house. Not so. The lease has expired.

So now I am homeless with four pups. All this stress, which I created for myself, could have been avoided. I could have done more research on how long construction takes and then added a few months for safety. I could have secured a longer lease on the temporary house. I could have waited to rescue the dogs until I was firmly ensconced in my house. When I analyze *why* I made these decisions, I realize it came down to impulsivity caused by anxiety. I was feeling upset about something work related and began all these projects to distract myself.

It's fine to redo your house, and it's fine to adopt dogs, but these are decisions that should be made with much more careful consideration than I gave them. Had I not been anxious and impulsive, I wouldn't be uprooted and could have managed all the situations seamlessly.

My lesson learned for the next time? When I am feeling upset, feel the upset. There is no getting around it; it's going to come out. And should I choose to engage in a project as a coping mechanism, then I must not be impulsive about it. I need to do the proper research to avoid as many stress-inducing hassles as possible.

WORKING IT OUT: WHAT'S YOUR PROBLEM?

I want you to take a moment here and write down all the problems that are plaguing you at this moment, from big to small. Now ask yourself what you contributed in creating your current situation. Did the professor fail you because you never went to class? Did your boss yell at you because you were on YouTube instead of working? Did your girlfriend leave you because you spent more time watching football with the guys than hanging out with her? Did you get mugged because you were hanging out in a bad part of town? Are you one hundred pounds overweight because you are rebelling against your parents for being critical when you were a kid? Did you attract the guy who treats you bad because you are playing out your unhealthy dynamic with your father? Were you diagnosed with lung cancer because you smoked like a chimney for twenty years?

I'm sure I seem unsympathetic here, but I guess that's because I am . . . if you do nothing to change your circumstances. At some point you have to stop acting as though life is happening to you and acknowledge the ways you are happening to it. Once you take responsibility for your side of the street, you grant yourself the power to improve every aspect of your life by simply acting and behaving differently. So do yourself a favor. Wake up already, pay attention, take responsibility, and learn life's lessons sooner rather than later so you don't keep making the same mistakes.

QUIZ
Are You a Victim or Victor?

CHAPTER SIX

GET AN ATTITUDE ADJUSTMENT

Once you have taken responsibility for the things you have done to create your current situation—and forgiven yourself for it, as you're only human!—it's time to start the slow and sometimes scary process of laying the real foundation for change.

I can lay out a step-by-step plan of action for you to follow to reach your goal, but unless you do the internal work, you won't get anywhere. Your attitudes and beliefs create your reality. What you perceive to be true becomes your reality. And so if you are going to change your reality, you have to give your attitude an overhaul from the ground up. This chapter will deal with your inner 'tude; after that we're on to the outside realm.

INNER 'TUDE

You may have seen me on *Loser* screaming furiously at contestants who let the words "I can't" pass their lips. Okay, yes, I scream at them for a lot of things. But seriously, "I can't" really pisses me off. Why? Because if you say it, you believe it, and it's a self-fulfilling prophecy. But flip it around, and the same is true of saying "I can."

It's true at every level: you attract what you focus on, and you achieve what you believe. If you are constantly saying to yourself that you can't, that you're not good enough, that you're a born failure, then that's the reality that you're going to make for yourself.

I'm not talking about the law of attraction, or any of the mystical magic of quantum mechanics I discussed in Chapter 3. I'm talking about the hard-core reality that your thoughts affect your behaviors, and your behaviors create your reality. This principle applies to every aspect of your life. So gearing your thought process into an "I can" mentality, and steering your mind away from fear-based scenarios, are critical.

Let me give you a few examples. Suppose you have a boyfriend (or girlfriend) who is controlling and doesn't give you any freedom. He makes you feel suffocated. So then you don't want to share any information with him, but that makes him even more insecure and controlling. Or suppose you have a boss who undervalues and mistrusts his employees. In turn, his employees steal from him, half-ass their jobs, or quit—because they have no loyalty to such a person and feel that turnabout is fair play. Or suppose you have an ultra-needy friend who never knows when to stop talking or when to leave. People avoid her like the plague, making her feel more alone and thus more needy. I've seen people running on the treadmill who say "I can't," then get so panicked and unfocused, they trip and injure themselves, creating a scenario where they *literally* can't.

We create what we fear. On some level I think we do it on purpose. We manifest our fears because they hold our deepest life lessons. And if we don't realize this, then we will never arrive at a place of triumph where we are able to beat our fears. This can significantly affect the quality of our lives.

Here's a fear I struggle with: I can be kind of high-strung sometimes, especially when it comes to work. One of my big anxiety triggers is feeling out of the loop—it brings up major issues about control and trust for me. But in the past, when my business partner would fill me in to put me in the loop, I would stress out about every little thing. So he stopped filling me in on the day-to-day stuff so I wouldn't freak out on him. But knowing he was keeping me out of the loop on purpose just made me more freaked out. It was a whole crazy cycle. So we made a deal: he would tell me everything, but the second I started to freak out, he'd stop. Now he will point out my behavior, remind me of our arrangement, and literally give me a time-out. I will take five minutes, do some deep breathing, get my anxiety in check, and then come back to the conversation with a level head. By implementing this arrangement, I took responsibility for the fact that my anxiety can get in my way, then put a game plan in place to control my anxiety, maintain focus, and power through. Get it?

Part of our work is to learn to look at the bigger lesson. I learned from this episode that I need to work on trusting people and releasing some amount of control. If I could do that, I'd get much more done in a day, and it would probably add years to my life.

Have you noticed that most things you are afraid of come to pass? If you fear being alone, are you perpetually single? If you fear being overweight, do you find it impossible to stop overeating? If you are afraid of being broke, do you find yourself constantly struggling to make ends meet? This exercise is meant to show you that your behavior is at the root of all self-fulfilling prophecies. There is no magic to the way things manifest in life. Ninety-nine percent of the time it's our conduct and our actions that create our circumstances. It's not bad luck or serendipity— all these things are a direct result of our attitude and thought processes.

NOTHING TO FEAR BUT FEAR ITSELF

One of my *Biggest Loser* contestants was terrified of getting hurt by his fiancée. All through his childhood his father told him never to trust women. (His father had undergone a terrible divorce.) Well, his warnings had a major impact on this contestant. He fell in love with a lovely woman but became panicked she would betray or hurt him. He might have expressed his feelings to her about his fears and insecurities; she could have reassured him, and they could have worked through his issues together. Instead he reacted unconsciously and began sabotaging the relationship. He acted as if he were indifferent to her and withdrew emotionally, so he would not get too invested in her and would be shielded from heartbreak if she ever did leave. Ultimately, his behavior created the very thing he feared the most: she left him. He was and still is devastated.

Here's another story for you. Lisa was a contestant on the *Biggest Loser* ranch. She was constantly talking about how she hated it and wanted to go home, yet she wasn't losing weigh-ins or falling below the line. Leaving *Biggest Loser* is easy—you can literally walk out the door, or you can have a crappy weigh-in, fall below the line, and get voted out. But she never did either of these things.

Well, I got sick of hearing her complaints, so I confronted her. "Why do you keep saying you want to leave, but then don't back it up by actually leaving? Don't you know how many people would kill to be here? What is this behavior of yours?"

It took some badgering, but I finally got the answer out of her. She didn't want to leave *Biggest Loser* at all—she wanted to stay more than anything. But she was feeling out of control. There was so much game playing going on that she felt she wouldn't be able to stay. If she actually got sent home, she would be devastated, so she began to "protect herself" by saying things like "I hate it here. I can't wait to leave. I just want to go home." She was rejecting the rejecter. It's a textbook defense mechanism where we convince ourselves we don't like the person who we feel is rejecting us in order to avoid feeling disappointment or loss.

But rejecting the rejecter is NOT a productive thing to do, and here's why. By constantly saying she hated *Biggest Loser* and wanted to go home, Lisa annoyed everyone: we trainers, the other contestants, and the show's producers. So if Lisa ever did fall below the line, she would likely be the first to be voted off. Eventually, that's exactly what happened.

While you cannot control what other people do, you can display certain attitudes and behaviors that influence things in your favor or against it. If Lisa had focused solely on her desire to be on the *Biggest Loser* ranch, she would have put her energy into her diet and her exercise regimen. She probably would have stayed above the line and would not have been eliminated. If she had taken a different attitude about her experience, and professed her desire to stay and get healthy, the other contestants might have voted someone else out instead of her. This is just another example of how we manifest our apprehensions and anxieties.

WORKING IT OUT

WHAT ARE YOU AFRAID OF?

Write down your innermost fears and insecurities. This will help you make the connections between what you fear and what you live.

Look at your present circumstances, and list some of your current problems. Really ruminate on them. Take a deep inventory of your life. For example:

Did someone leave you?
Did your kids rebel against you?
Did your boss fire you?
Did your coworkers reject you?

These questions are just a few obvious ones about how we manifest deep primal fears. Your fear doesn't have to be about your deepest insecurities. The overall point is for you to look at how you create your reality, from the big to the small. Take my friend whose dog needed the expensive surgery, and it crushed his finances. I'm sure that his dog's illness wasn't one of his biggest fears—at least until it happened. But had he been more conscientious and responsible with pet insurance, he could have avoided taking that massive financial hit.

WHAT IN YOUR LIFE IS NOT WORKING FOR YOU?

List all the things that are currently out of whack in your life. I have listed a few more random examples in the event that you still aren't getting it—even though I am pretty sure you are.

> Did you get hurt in your exercise class?
> Did you have a fight with your spouse?
> Did you bounce a check?
> Did you wreck your car?

Look at what you're doing to contribute to those scenarios. How could your behavior be creating your existing problems?

Now I want you to break down all the interactions you have or don't have with people on a daily basis, and examine how you approach every situation, person, place, or thing that intimidates, upsets, overwhelms, or scares you.

**QUIZ
Do You
Need an
Attitude
Adjustment?**

> Do you get defensive?
> Do you get cocky and arrogant?
> Do you reject the rejecter?
> Do you become overly controlling and determined to overcome the problem at hand?
> Do you become anxious, impulsive, or flustered?
> Do you do things to distract yourself that end up causing chaos (like rescuing several dogs when you are momentarily homeless)?

Do you rebel and cause more damage out of spite (like binge-eating to get back at your parents for not loving you unconditionally)?

Do you numb out and neglect necessary day-to-day responsibilities, like getting car insurance or pet insurance, or making doctors' appointments?

Follow me? Recognize your part in creating the problems that keep sabotaging you. Remember how I recognized that my freak-outs were making it impossible for my business partner to keep me up to date about things (which is what I needed him to do to prevent me from freaking out). You are the only person who can end your own crazy cycles of self-destruction. Recognize them for what they are; take this time to pinpoint as many of yours as you can.

JUST STOP!

Once you have identified your contributions to the self-defeating patterns in your life, you have to stop them and implement replacement behaviors.

As soon as you see yourself starting to fall back into an old behavior, STOP. Take a step back or a deep breath—whatever you need to do to slow yourself down and become conscious of what you are doing. Before you act, put yourself through a little consciousness exercise. Think about your goal, and how the behavior you're about to engage in will help or delay its achievement. How can you adjust your behavior and your attitude to better serve you?

If you know that when you feel lonely, you become insanely needy and pester your friends until they want to lose your phone number, then think of something you can do to counteract that loneliness before it sabotages your relationships. Go for a jog to get your endorphins pumping, so you feel strong and capable. Pick up a hobby or project that you are passionate about, and lose yourself in it for a couple of hours. Consider adopting a pet (but not when you are out of house and home).

IT'S A REACH

When you are feeling vulnerable and fearing rejection, rather than rejecting the other person or situation and shutting down, try reaching out instead. If a guy flakes out on you for a date, don't play games and not return his call for two days. That only breeds more game playing, which gets the two of you nowhere. Instead tell him that you really like him, but it hurt your feelings when he canceled, and it felt disrespectful. If he can't respect that and change his ways, then you know he is not a person for you to be dating, and you can move on. Most likely he'll apologize and tell you that he likes you as well and didn't realize it hurt your feelings, and that in the future he will make efforts to keep his plans with you.

It's scary to expose our feelings and open ourselves up, so it will take time to adopt these new behaviors. But you will realize that it's the only way to build true intimacy and a fulfilled, enriched life. And even if you are rejected, you'll survive it with the knowledge that you cleaned up your side of the street and did the right thing.

SWAP IT OUT

Maybe you're the kind of person who, when anxious, obsesses and reacts impulsively in ways that only add fuel to the fire. If so, then think of something you can do in response to anxiety so you don't make matters worse. Take a bubble bath, go for a half-hour massage on your lunch hour, try journaling, or do something comforting and gentle. But you must counteract the anxiety so that you can stop your problematic self-destructive behavior in its tracks.

You could do what my editor does—go kick and punch someone—but only in a contained environment, and only if you're sparring. Take a kickboxing class or study martial arts. Not only will it help you feel empowered and strong, but it will also help you "kick" that anxiety to the curb.

In Step Three, which is all about action, we'll get into things you can do to stay on track in a lot more detail. But I want you to start seeing now how all the advice I'm giving is tied together; I've crafted the plan so that you can rely on every part of it to help you get out of your own way and create the life you deserve.

ROLE CALL

Another way we limit ourselves is by boxing ourselves into roles we think we're supposed to be playing. We are all the main character in the movie or novel of our lives, whether we like to admit it or not. At some point we assign ourselves a role based on the patterns we have been playing out since childhood: we're the victim, we're the martyr, the hero, the dumb pretty one, the smart ugly one, the nice guy who never gets the girl, blah blah blah. You know what I'm talking about.

Well, it's time to throw those roles out the window. They're nothing more than constructs that our imagination created from other people's issues and that we internalized in childhood. Although they seem real in your head, they are NOT REALITY, and they limit our lives in unforgiving ways.

Your self-confidence comes largely from your self-image. And your self-image and your role in the world dictate what you expect of yourself and for yourself. If you have a negative story, then you automatically assume a negative future.

Your experiences and memories define your self-image. If you had a critical parent who was always driving you toward perfection because inside he or she felt imperfect, you might have internalized their insecurities, so that you think you are never good enough. You approach your life believing that nothing you do will ever be up to par. This self-image begets more experiences of inadequacy, in a vicious cycle that continues in perpetuity. So here we are back with the self-fulfilling prophecies again. You achieve what you believe. There is no variation on this truth. If you embrace limiting stories, you will play out the same scenario for the rest of your life—*until* you wake up and say enough is enough.

It is the prison of your mind that causes your suffering, not the dead-end job or the loveless relationship—those are merely symptoms of your character's story.

It's not easy to change the way you see yourself. If you grew up experiencing loss, failure, or rejection, or believing that you're lazy, or a loser, or whatever—it's hard to break those beliefs because you don't have any other frame of reference. But I swear to you, whatever limiting ideas you have about yourself are not true. At some early point you took on this story, for whatever reason, and it repeated itself because you believed it to be true.

There's an anecdote I came across in a self-help book years ago that I have never forgotten, and it really underlines what I'm talking about:

A father and his young son are at the circus. The son sees a huge elephant shackled with flimsy, rusted chains. Turning to his dad, he asks, "Isn't that elephant strong enough to break free from those chains?"

"Of course he is," his dad answers. "It's just that he's been chained like that since he was too small and weak to break free, and now he doesn't know the difference."

I hate to say it, but buddy, you are the elephant in this story.

You CAN leave the job you hate. You CAN leave the alcoholic spouse. You CAN go back to school. Want to know what's holding you back? Absolutely nothing but you!

WORKING IT OUT: BREAKING FREE OF LIMITATIONS

Here are a couple more questions to help you break free from the limitations you may be placing on yourself without even realizing it:

WHAT'S YOUR STORY?

What is your role in your own life story, and how is it imprisoning you and holding you back? Are you fat because you think you're lazy? Are you poor because you think you're a loser? Are you staying in a dead-end job because you think it's too late to change careers? Are you alone because you think you're not special enough to find someone to love you? I have to stop before I scream, "Not true!" But you get the idea. Write down all the ways in which your self-definitions keep you from the life you want.

IS IT A TRUE STORY?

Is there any truth whatsoever to your story? Think long and hard about it. Are you physically incapable of walking out the door and filing for divorce? If you're staying for the sake of the children, consider this: kids know when they are in an unhappy home. Ultimately, it may be better for them if you remove yourself from a bad marriage.

Are you really too lazy to start an exercise regime and lose weight? That's doubtful. Are you really too much of a loser to earn money? Probably not. Are you *really* too old to go on job interviews or go back to school? Um, not unless you are like 103. Are you some kind of freak that no one on earth could ever love? NO!!

These are just examples. Whatever your self-imposed limitations may be, now is the time to identify them so you can kiss them goodbye. You need to tell a new story, preferably one where you are living a passionate, meaningful life, full of love and vintage muscle cars.

And don't go telling me it's complicated, because it's not; it's simple. All it requires are a few new ideas and a few courageous steps to put your life back on track. Will it be easy? Hell, no! That is a false promise I won't make you. But it's *totally* possible and utterly worth it. Seeing the fallacies that are at the root of your negative self-image is the only way to free yourself to live your higher calling.

THE ART OF FAKING IT

Your self-image is the crucial factor in where your journey takes you. And it is never neutral; it either moves you forward or holds you back. If you believe yourself to be a worthless failure, the decisions and choices you make will come from that belief, and you will probably end up failing. Believe the opposite, and yes, that too is what you will get.

Once you understand this fact, you are free to find new attitudes and beliefs about yourself, which will in turn change the choices you make and the results you achieve. It's going to take time and practice—you can't change your self-image overnight. But keep working the steps of this program, and it will get easier. The small victories and successes that you achieve through educated, determined diligence will dramatically help you to redefine your self-image.

On *Biggest Loser,* when I take a contestant who thinks she is lazy and weak into the gym, put her through a grueling two-hour workout, and maybe get her to run her first mile, she instantly becomes a new person. (It's true for male contestants, too.) In that moment she experiences a new reality, one where she is strong and accomplished. In that short time her backstory is shattered, and a world of possibility opens up to her. She realizes that if the belief that she is weak and lazy isn't true, then other self-defeating ideas and beliefs that she has been holding on to may also be untrue. From this place of possibility the sky becomes the limit.

Now, presuming that these small successes and victories will take time to manifest and germinate, you'll have to "fake it till you make it."

You must've heard that one before. Try it. The reason it works is that if you keep taking positive action, before long it becomes habit, and eventually you will believe in it. It's sort of a cart-before-the-horse thing, but it WORKS. With the right course of action—education, time, practice, and patience—you will be successful. And confidence in success begets success. But more on that action front later. We've dealt with your inner 'tude—now it's time for a look at your view as you look out.

CHAPTER SEVEN

OUTER 'TUDE

We've been talking a lot about your attitude toward yourself. But what about your attitude toward life and the world around you? How do you handle the curveballs life throws you? When something bad happens, do you choose to learn from it and gain depth and insight? Or do you allow it to crush you, seeing the defeat as validation that you do, in fact, suck?

Learning to transform your negative attitudes doesn't stop with your inner view—you also have to be honest about how your attitudes about the outside world are holding you back.

It is possible to take an adversity and turn it into an opportunity for success. And I'm not talking "glass half full" crap. I'm talking about literally rewiring your internal circuitry and shifting the way you see the world, so you are resilient and programmed to survive any failure, blast through every obstacle, and overcome any setback.

Let's address some of the most common pitfalls we can stumble into as we navigate and interact with the world around us: worry, fear, and failure.

QUIT YOUR WORRYING

Anxiety is *useless*. It serves absolutely no purpose except to rob you of valuable energy that could instead be channeled into creating your new life. Seriously, you tell me what good can come from worry and stress. I don't know about you, but I can do without sleepless nights and high blood pressure and sweaty palms and tension headaches. They just make everything worse. I've struggled with anxiety my whole life and have learned a few things about how to knock it out.

PRESENT!

Root yourself firmly in the present moment. Often when we flip out, the thing we're flipping out about is something we fear will happen in the future. Anticipation is scarier in many cases than reality. Very often the thing we're so worried about never even happens, and if it does, all the advance worrying in the world won't make it any better.

So when you start to stress out, ask yourself how things really are right now. At this moment, do you have a job? At this moment, are you healthy? Are you getting by financially, and is there a roof over your head? Are your loved ones alive and well?

Sure, bad things might happen. I'm not saying you should go into major head-in-the-sand denial about that possibility. Nor am I saying you shouldn't plan ahead and take necessary precautions to safeguard yourself and your loved ones. What I'm getting at is that you can't let problems that don't yet exist ruin your life. Remember the old saying "Cross that bridge when you come to it." Or better yet, as my company's producing partner Ellen Rakieten always tells me, "Don't bleed until you're shot." If and when a bad thing happens, you will manage the situation as productively as possible, but until then, stay present and deal with the task, and moment, at hand.

BE A RESOURCEFUL MOUSE

When a problem arises, it's important to focus on the solution, not the problem itself. There's a great book you may have heard about called *Who Moved My Cheese?* The title comes from an experiment conducted with mice in mazes. Every day for weeks the mice would run through their mazes and find a piece of cheese in the same place. Then one day the researchers moved the cheese. Some of the mice had little mouse freak-outs. They went to where the cheese had been and scratched at the walls and paced around in circles. Because they were so busy freaking out, they never found the cheese in its new location. In real life this would have meant starvation and death, otherwise known as *exactly the thing the mouse was freaking out about.*

Now, some of the other mice reacted completely differently. When they didn't find the cheese where they expected to, they took a beat and then retraced their steps, sniffed around, and experimented with alternate routes until they found it.

Which mouse are you going to be?

Are you going to stress out and shut down? Or are you going to use your skills and resources to find a solution? The second one is the right answer.

Your first step is to reduce the problem to its simplest form. If you're worried about catching swine flu because you have a chronic disease that puts you at greater risk for it, then Google it and research the measures you can take to protect yourself. Stay out of Mexico, where this flu originated, for one. Don't fly unless you have to do so, and take natural supplements to boost your immune system.

If you're scared you might lose your job, focus on doing better at work. Or if that part is out of your control and layoffs are abounding at your workplace, then start searching the want ads and hitting the pavement and filling out job applications.

Being proactive is a major stress buster. If you really think about it, there are small steps you can take to keep the bad things from happening, or to deal with them when they do. Once you have exhausted all your proactive options, you can look for ways to calm your mind.

GIVE YOUR BRAIN A BOOST

Find activities that relieve your stress, behaviors that release mood-enhancing serotonin. They'll help distract you so you don't turn the situation over and over again in your head. 'Cuz that's what obsessive crazy people do. I know—I was one. I spent years as a congenital worrier—and I always worried best between midnight and four A.M. It was not fun or remotely productive.

There are lots of things you can do to temporarily take yourself away from your stress. Exercising. Deep-breathing techniques. Any activity that you enjoy and that is life affirming: gardening, knitting, working on your car. If you love it and it calms you down, do more of it! Whenever I get super-stressed, and I've already done everything I can to proactively attack the situation head-on, I go for a ride on my horse or take a spin on my motorcycle. Find the activities that nurture your soul and occupy your mind, that take you to a "happy place," so that you can prevent your anxiety from crippling you.

If this isn't enough to convince you, then ask yourself: if a beloved friend or family member came to you stressed out, scared, or beating themselves up over something, what would you do? Most likely you'd tell them everything's going to be okay. You might suggest they take a long hot bath. You might give them a massage. You might send loving texts and reassuring e-mails throughout the day. You wouldn't emotionally beat the crap out of them. (At least I hope not.) So why the hell wouldn't you do the exact same thing for yourself?! For some reason a lot of us think it's soft or self-indulgent to be kind to ourselves. Actually, learning to be loving and nurturing toward yourself will help you come through every hardship stronger and wiser.

GET A SECOND OPINION

I bet you've heard the old saying "You can't see the forest for the trees." (I just love clichés. They remind us just how obvious and simple most of life can be—if we let it.) Well, very often when we're stressed out about a situation, we are too close to it to have any real perspective. It helps to get a second pair of eyes to look at the landscape. Reaching out to someone for advice is beneficial emotionally as well as strategically. Not only will you feel supported and not alone in your predicament (we can all use that from time to time), but you will also get a calmer, cooler picture of your situation from someone who is not attached or engaged the way you are.

When we are too emotionally fired up about a situation, we can't assess it realistically or take rational, productive action. If you reach out to someone who isn't personally involved in or attached to it, you can vent, process, weigh options, and basically get your head straight so you can decide on a course of action—even if that action is to be still for the moment and do nothing.

A quick caveat: be mindful of whom you approach for this second opinion. If you have a friend who agrees with everything you say, that's probably not a great person for you to mull things over with. Be thoughtful about whom you seek advice from. We will discuss this in greater detail in Chapter 9, but for now seek out someone you trust who has a calm, cool head, preferably with some knowledge of the situation you are mulling over.

These are a few ways to help you release your worries, anxieties, and inner conflicts, so you can stop them from sapping your energy, and free yourself for things that are much more productive and rewarding. Worry is begotten by fear, and fear is one of the biggest saboteurs out there, so that's what we're going to tackle next.

USE YOUR FEAR TO MAKE YOU STRONGER

There are hundreds of books out there that tout "fearlessness." The word alone conjures images of human beings defying the laws of nature, doesn't it? It just sounds so cool! Well, you can forget about becoming fearlesss—don't even bother trying! Every living thing, from the smallest insect to the most powerful CEO, feels fear. It's at the very core of nature, so if you think you can escape it, think again. The trick is not to escape your fears but to confront and use them to drive and teach you. Only by getting to the bottom of your fears can you find their valuable lessons and move forward stronger than before.

Fear can lead you straight to panic and confusion, or to clarity and meaning. It can paralyze and destroy you, or it can be your greatest source of motivation. I've seen it bring out the very worst in people (myself included!), and I've also seen it drive people to overcome the most extraordinary obstacles (I'm going to include myself here, as well). Quite possibly one of the greatest achievements in life is to learn how to let your fear guide you to clarity rather than to madness. Believe it or not, it's entirely up to you.

Here are two examples from my own life. In the first one I let fear motivate me negatively, and in the second one I let fear motivate me for the best.

In the past, relationships were *not* my strong point. I have struggled with intimacy issues my whole life, and I'm still working them out. But looking back I realize that there was one relationship in particular that I sabotaged out of fear. I was a lot younger than I am now, and I was dating someone who was older than me. I was intimidated by that and acted immaturely in the relationship. I would stop communicating and become cold, because I didn't want to seem weak or needy. I was constantly afraid that this person would hurt me, so I shut down. And ultimately that brought the relationship to its end. If I had been brave enough to voice my feelings of insecurity, to communicate my needs, then it might have worked out differently. But I didn't see that then. I know now that to find happiness, you have to open yourself up to let it in. As I'm sure you know from your own life experiences, fear that is not handled properly can shut you down and keep you from finding the happiness you deserve.

Now for the positive example.

When I was in my twenties, I had a handful of friends whose parents continued to support them years after college. I was so jealous, thinking how lucky they were not to have to worry constantly about paying rent, buying groceries, or putting a little gas in the car. These friends now, though, have achieved almost nothing with their lives. They are apathetic and unmotivated because life has been too comfortable. They were never forced to work, so they've never had to think about what their purpose is, what fulfills them. They never learned the social skills to forge connections and put together careers. They didn't build the mental stamina and physical endurance that comes from a strong work ethic. Now they're all in their midthirties, and still wondering what the hell they're about.

On the other hand, I was pretty much on my own from the age of seventeen. My mom gave me $400 a month toward rent till I was eighteen, and she paid for my therapy until I was twenty-four. (I've already made it clear: she thought that was pretty important, God love her.) But that was it. So I was *forced* to deal with my fear of having nothing. I had to hustle to find work, cope with rejection at job interviews, and learn the skills of communicating and establishing relationships. I had to try different things because my livelihood literally depended on it. Did I get myself into some tough spots? You bet. But I learned how to get myself out of them, too, and now I see exactly what my mother was doing with her tough-love approach.

Having to make it without any help taught me how to channel fear and use it to fight my way forward.

FIGHT NIGHT

Here is one more example, from my martial arts training. (If you've heard me tell this story before, tough. It's appropriate for my point, so I'll regale you with it one more time.) I was about thirteen, and my parents' divorce was not even a year old. I had recently lost my beloved grandmother to lung cancer. I was still a heavy kid and very much the "victim" in school. In fact, I was feeling like a victim in my life. So I was not in a good head space. One day I was sparring with my martial arts instructor on what we called "fight night." (A bunch of the students and black belts would get together and spar.) I was basically a beginner, maybe a blue belt, and I figured he was not really going to hit me hard. It was just practice training. After all, I was a novice *and* a kid going through a tough time—right? Wrong.

Suddenly I found myself in a corner getting the crap kicked out of me. Literally one sidekick after another was being delivered right into my stomach. With the wind knocked out of me, I immediately curled into a ball, took cover, and started crying. To my amazement, he did not stop kicking me. Instead he said, "Life is not going to stop knocking the wind out of you. You can pull it together and fight your way out of that corner, or I can break your ribs." And then he delivered another swift blow to my solar plexus. I promise you this is no exaggeration.

But in that moment I realized that I couldn't allow fear to immobilize me. I had to use it as motivation to fight back—and I did. That night I fought my way out of the corner, and I have been doing it ever since.

Life is not fair, rational, or reasonable. It doesn't matter who you are or what you are going through—life is merciless, and it's up to you to either move through fear and rise to life's terrifying occasions or curl up in a ball and let life beat you down. The decisions we make at these pivotal crossroads define our lives and weave the story of our existence.

If you learn how to manage fear, how to embrace it, feel it, weigh your course of action in response to it, and then take deliberate steps to move through it and out of it, it can be an amazing source of power.

SPARE SOME CHANGE?

Our most destructive fear, one that we all wrestle with, is the fear of change—which is, ironically, the very thing we yearn for the most. Although we all want more out of life, we're scared of anything that might place us in unknown territory: gaining weight or losing weight, failing or succeeding, getting sick or having a loved one get sick, leaving a dead-end relationship, losing a job, getting old. The list is endless because when you fear change, you fear everything. And by resisting change, you stunt your evolution. Even though change is the only constant in life, we cling to the status quo. Fear is really an indication that you are moving toward change, so it's really only a natural part of your journey.

Eleanor Roosevelt said, "You should do something every day that scares you." Moving into the unknown opens you up to the infinite possibilities that are out there for you. Suppose you are in an unhealthy relationship and you stay in it because you are terrified of being alone. If you can overcome your fear and leave, you open up the emotional space for someone new, someone better to come along. Suppose you've left a job that made you miserable, or you've been fired, and you're terrified about how you're going to make money. If you can overcome your fear, you can seek out new opportunities, and you might just end up with a better gig.

So don't run from your fears. You'll end up running into a wall and getting nowhere.

Since I can't put this any better myself, here's a quote that illustrates my point:

> **"Life is perverse in the sense that the more you seek security, the less of it you have. But the more you seek opportunity, the more likely it is that you will achieve the security that you desire."**
> —BRIAN TRACY, INSPIRATIONAL SPEAKER AND AUTHOR

Have faith. By allowing yourself to be pulled toward the unknown, you create space, literally and figuratively, for good things to come in and shape your life. And that's what we're here for, after all.

The scariest moments in our lives are the ones where we have the greatest opportunities to learn and evolve, so get comfortable with the idea of being a little uncomfortable.

Here's a spoiler: your fears *will* come to pass.

You will fall on your ass, and you will be rejected. Bad things happen to good people all the time. But so what? You've had setbacks in the past, and clearly you've survived them. With the right attitude and a few strategies, you can retool your fear mechanisms so that they're working for you rather than against you. Here are a few exercises to help you build your tolerance for fear, especially fear of the unknown.

WRESTLING WITH DEMONS

Often we fear that our own actions will lead to a catastrophic result. This fear can overwhelm you and shut you down, causing you to go into denial and run from your issues. Fear, however, cannot be outrun. Running only makes the situation snowball; the more you run, the bigger the monster gets. Instead, give yourself permission to be afraid. Play out, in your head, the absolute worst thing that could happen, all the way to the very end. Most of the time you will realize that your fear is not based in reality, or that its possible fulfillment is not truly that bad. By exploring your fears in depth, you can analyze the real risks, quiet the irrational aspects, and face what remains head-on.

WORKING IT OUT

Take a moment to write down the thing you fear most in life at this very moment.

Now make a list of all the things that would happen if your fear came true.

Ask yourself, are these things really *that* awful? Would you still be thinking about them next month, next year, or in five years? Are they unfixable in the long run?

WHAT'S THE WORST THAT COULD HAPPEN?

Here's an example of playing out the worst-case scenario for a fear. A friend of mine was terrified to ask out a girl he liked at work. He really, really liked her, but he simply couldn't bring himself to approach her. So I sat down with him, and we went through all the possible outcomes together, calmly and rationally. (Okay, I was the calm and rational one, so you know that the guy had it bad.) The conversation went something like this:

Him: What if I ask her out and she's not into me?
Me: What are the consequences of that in your life?
Him: None, but I'd have to see her at work every day.
Me: So?
Him: Well, it's embarrassing and the whole office will know.
Me: Is that embarrassment going to kill you?
Him: No.
Me: Is it something you can't get over?
Him: No.
Me: Do you really care what the people in your office think about
     anything other than your work?
Him: Yes.
Me: Why?
Him: Because I want them to like me. I want things at work to be
     comfortable.

Me: You are projecting your insecurities onto strangers. If the people in your office think less of you because you asked someone out and didn't get a positive outcome, are those the people you want in your life anyway? Seriously. Do you want to surround yourself with judgmental people who don't love or support you when you're feeling down or vulnerable?

Him: No.

Me: Plus, you have true friends. A true friend would support you in that situation and not judge you. I am supporting you and will continue to support you. When people show you who they really are by judging you unfairly, that is a favor they're doing you, and you have to pay attention.

Him: Right, I get that.

Me: So what do you really have to lose? You will take a quick blow to the ego—that's the worst-case scenario. And what's that saying? A bad day for the ego is a good day for the soul. It's true. You will get the benefit of learning a little more about who the people you work with really are, which will help you make informed decisions about who you let into your life. And don't you think the possibility of things working out in your favor is worth the risk of a little embarrassment? Plus, the kind of emotional stretching that comes with facing fear allows you to gain strength in future endeavors where you'll need courage.

Him: Okay, I see your point. I will take the chance and talk to her tomorrow.

By mapping out the scenario step by step, he was able to weigh the pros and cons rationally. Not only did this preparation help him emotionally for the worst case if it should come to pass, but it also helped him realize how much of his fear was unfounded or negligible compared with the possible reward.

Other than death, there's NOTHING we can't rebound from. And with a little resilience we can and will come out the other end stronger, wiser, and readier than ever to live at our best.

WHAT'S THE BEST-CASE SCENARIO?

People don't generally run toward uncomfortable situations, so another great way to push through fear is to determine the reward that could await you. There is no fear that you can't overcome if the outcome is worth the risk. Review the fears you wrote down before. But now, instead of imagining all the bad things that could happen, imagine just the opposite, and think of all the great possibilities that could play out.

Let's go back to my friend with the office crush.

Me: Why do you want to ask this girl out?

Him: I think she's beautiful. She's charming, funny, and smart. She always makes everyone in the office smile.

Me: Okay, so if you ask her and she *doesn't* laugh at you, then what happens?

Him: I guess we go on a date.

Me: Then what happens?

Him: I don't know . . .

Me: No. Don't go to a place of "I don't know," or fear. Play it out.

Him: We go out. We hit it off. She turns out to be the one. We get married. Have two kids. Live happily ever after.

Me: Wow. Sounds pretty nice. Do you think the possibility of gaining all that is worth risking being turned down or embarrassed in front of a bunch of people you barely know?

Him: Yes, of course. But it's more than that. If she says no, I'll be crushed. Now you've got me wanting to marry this girl! The disappointment will be devastating.

Me: Look, the disappointment is *already* devastating you, and you haven't even asked her out yet. Right now you have nothing. This girl is not yours. You're not dating. For all we know you're not even on her radar. How can it get more disappointing than that, if what you really want is to be with her?

Him: Well, at least at the moment we're friends. If I ask her out and she says no, then it will be awkward, and we won't even be cool with each other around the office.

Me: No! That is not the case unless you make it so. If you ask her out and she says no, the way things go from there depends on your actions and your behavior. If she says no and you're sweet and kind about it and laugh it off, no matter how you feel inside, the awkwardness will pass, and you'll remain friends. Yes, you'll be disappointed, but you can talk about that with your friends who love you, with people like me. You deal with it with us, and then you can remain normal with her. Your being weird around her is the only thing that will make her weird around you.

Him: You have a point.

Yes, the unknown can be scary, even painful at times. But venturing into it is usually worth the risk. Even if the outcome isn't what you'd hoped for, you will still take away valuable lessons that can help you grow in other areas of your life. Remember, every action you take plants a seed; if you take that action with a pure intention, it will yield fruit in time. Oh, by the way, my friend from the anecdote above is engaged to the girl. I just love a happy ending.

WALK IN SOMEONE ELSE'S SHOES

There are people in this world who have lived through the very thing you fear. I guarantee it.

How did they pull through? What did they do to turn things around? And what could they have done better?

Stories are a powerful way to effect change, both in others and in ourselves. By closely studying the stories of people who have survived or conquered the thing you fear, you can create a vicarious intellectual and emotional experience of success that will empower you to push through. I use this method a lot when I work with people. For example, on *Biggest Loser* I make a point of telling them all about my own struggles with body image and weight loss. I walk them through my journey from the beginning to where I am right now. On an emotional level they become invested and go through the journey with me. And then in their moments of uncertainty, they think, *If Jillian can do it, so can I.*

A much more powerful example is the show itself. I can't tell you how many people from around the world e-mail, write letters, write on my Facebook wall, and even come up to me on the street to tell me how much weight they have lost and how their lives have changed "because of the show." Now, you and I both know the show didn't lose the weight or change their lives. By watching the show, however, and identifying with the contestants, they went along for the ride as well. They felt the struggles and shared in the successes. If the contestants could do it, so could they. See how this works?

Knowing how someone else's shoes feel can help you get in step with your own. Let's use it to your advantage. Pick a person who has walked before you, and observe closely. If it's someone well known, read everything you can about them. If it's not, find out as much as you can through whatever means you can (no stalking, just pay attention). Study their path and their process, and imagine yourself in the same scenarios. Try to do so as vividly as possible.

This study will help you build a frame of reference for the unknown, so at some level it will become familiar terrain. By living it through someone else's experience, you will have practiced it mentally, and so when your time comes, you will be less afraid. You'll have a sense of guidance, almost an internal GPS. No two paths are exactly the same, but having a rudimentary map gives us confidence to forge ahead on our own.

COME ON, BUDDY

Pick someone in your life you admire. Your grandfather, an old college professor, a friend—it doesn't matter who, as long as you have total respect for them and you admire their life or accomplishments. Then when you're about to take a leap, visualize this person at your side, rooting for you, telling you how much they believe in you. Try it when you ask for a raise, or ask someone on a date, or go for a bank loan to start your small business, or do anything scary that takes you outside your comfort zone. We all need a little encouragement and support sometimes. I'm not saying this should be your sole source of motivation, or that you should be doing anything for other people's approval, but a little mental backup can go a long way.

And it really works. Whenever I'm going into a tough situation, I imagine my grandmother watching over me. I feel her with me. I hear her tell me how impressed she is with my courage, and that she loves me no matter what. This helps me push through whatever has me in the grip of fear, because I feel unconditionally loved and supported no matter what the outcome.

Managing your fear and conquering its crippling effects are going to be a part of your life's work—you can't do it all overnight. Rome wasn't built in a day and all that. Remember Eleanor Roosevelt's words, and get in there and do something that scares you.

By taking small, courageous steps, you stretch your emotional fabric and gradually push yourself out of your comfort zone. This will help you accept and get comfortable with the reality that life is unpredictable, change is constant, and risk is necessary if we're going to live up to our potential.

And yes, at times, you're going to fail. We all do it, and we all hate it—me included. But there is a silver lining to this dark cloud. And we've all heard it, though we don't often like it: failure is a far better teacher than success, and for that reason it is a necessary part of your journey. So next let's take a good hard look at failure.

PICK YOURSELF UP, DUST YOURSELF OFF . . .

Many people (maybe you're one of them) know they need to make a change, either personal or professional, but they don't

because they're terrified that if it doesn't work out, it will somehow mean the end of the world. Or they're afraid that if they
fail, it will confirm every dark thought they've ever had about
themselves—they'll finally have *proof* that they're not good
enough. Some of us worry that if we fail, our friends and loved
ones will think less of us, be disappointed in us, even withdraw
from us. I *know* some of you feel this way. Every single person I
have ever worked with feels this way. Hell, sometimes I feel this
way, and I'm the one writing the book!

Often we don't try because then we can't fail. This choice lets
us continue to believe in the possibility that we *might be* capable.
It at least lets us think that we have successfully hidden our weaknesses from others.

For example, many people who are overweight don't bother
trying to lose weight. They act as if they don't mind being heavy
and pretend they are happy with the way they are. In their heads,
they hang on to the belief that they could change if they really
wanted to. In truth, their greatest fear is that they will try and
fail, sending a message to others that they are weak and lazy and
confirming to themselves that they are incapable of change. If
they try to lose weight for health as well as happiness but fail,
they will be crushed and fear that they will be relegated to a life of
unhappiness and unhealthiness. For these reasons, most people
don't risk it—they live in a place I call the "comfortably numb." I
ripped off that phrase from a Pink Floyd song, and I find it utterly
appropriate. I use it all the time when describing the emotional
and psychological state of many people I work with, heavy or not.

But you can't selectively shut down your feelings. When you
numb out, the whole limbic system (the main area of the brain
responsible for emotions) goes down. You feel nothing. Not happiness, not sadness, not elation, not devastation—nothing!

In season six of *Biggest Loser* I met a beautiful young woman
called Coleen. As the result of one of the show's challenges, she
had backed herself into a corner—she and her dad *had* to lose a
collective fourteen pounds over the course of the week, or they

would face possible elimination. In our workouts that week I was pushing her and pushing her. At a certain point every time, she would just start crying and give up. So I got in her face. I asked her *why*, at the very moment when she needed to be trying the hardest, she was giving up. She broke down and said that it was because she'd never tried so hard for anything before. Again I asked her why, and she said the idea of failing was too terrifying. At that particular moment she realized how much she had to lose if she didn't give her *all*, so she was able to push through, and she went on to great success and triumph on the show.

Look, there are no two ways about it—failure SUCKS. It's hurtful, embarrassing, time-consuming, and soul-crushing; it makes you want to crawl into a hole and die. No wonder so many people think the smart option is to play it safe. *If I don't try, I can't get hurt*—sound familiar?

When you are contemplating taking a risk that could result in failure, the first thing you need to remember is that *you will have value whether you fail or succeed*. No one is judging you based solely on one failure. And if they are, thank them for showing you who they are, and then show them the door; you can now steer clear of them and keep their negative influence out of your life. Remember that we're all mirrors, and they're probably just projecting their own feelings of inadequacy onto you anyway. Bottom line, you don't have to let it in. Like a mirror, you can deflect it. And as for the judgment you put on yourself if you fail, that's also bullshit. In truth, by taking a risk you are stronger and braver than most. The only true failure is in not trying.

There's nothing fun about falling on your ass, but it's an essential part of your ascendance, both personally and professionally. You *will* fail. At least I hope so, because it will mean you are really living, really reaching. Failure teaches you how to succeed. When you learn what you've done wrong, you can take steps in the future to get it right. The key to overcoming failure is to use it as an entry point for learning, a way into wisdom. With the right attitude, you can transform any setback into a guide for growth.

Here's another story for you. About a year before I auditioned for *Biggest Loser,* I was up for a VH1 show called *Flab to Fab.* I desperately wanted the job. I went to the interview and killed it. I talked diet, fitness, psychology. I gave them everything they wanted to hear. I thought I was a shoo-in. All my celebrity clients called on my behalf to put in a good word. My clients knew I was the front-runner for the job, and so did all the other trainers in town. I'll cut to the chase and tell you what you've probably already figured out: I didn't get the job. I was *totally* humiliated. I thought my peers would revel in my failure. I thought my clients would see me as a loser and reconsider training with me. But neither of those things happened. Not even a little. Obviously, I had been projecting a deep insecurity inside myself onto others.

I took a week or so to nurse my bruised ego, then did a little nosing around to try to find out why I hadn't gotten the job. I had reservations at first; I didn't know what I was going to learn. I'd already been rejected, and to ask why was almost like rubbing salt into the wound. But I did it anyway because it was about more than my ego. It was about finding out where I had gone wrong and learning from my mistakes and excelling in future opportunities. And here's what I discovered: I didn't get the job because they thought my celebrity clientele would make me seem inaccessible to the public. As soon as I found that out, big bells went off—this was my lesson.

Have you ever seen me do an article or a TV segment about celebrity fitness? No, and you never will, because I figured out at that moment that it *does* send the wrong message to people. What I do isn't about getting you to look like a celebrity. It's about getting you to have *your* best body, not J-Lo's or Jennifer Aniston's, and it's about living *your* best life.

Then a year later *Loser* came up. I incorporated the lesson from my failure the year before and lined up testimonials from all my soccer moms, baby boomers, and average Joes. We all know how this story ends. *Flab to Fab* was on for only one season. Had I gotten that job, I would have been under contract and wouldn't have been free to audition for *Biggest Loser,* which has turned into an international platform for me to get my message of healthy and fulfilled living out to millions of viewers. To sum it up: I failed, I looked at why, and I made improvements so that the next time opportunity showed up, I was smarter and more prepared. And look where it got me.

With courage and honesty, you can and will turn failures into tools for success and vehicles for personal growth. The following exercises will guide you through the process. Some of these questions can be painful and horribly uncomfortable to answer—but you know by now that that's just a sign that you're doing it right.

WORKING IT OUT

Did you lose that job because you were late so often? Do you need to work on your communication skills? Did you mess up a work presentation because you left it till the last minute? Examining what went wrong will guide you specifically to what you need to work on. Don't be scared. This stuff can really hit the ego, hard. But you will grow stronger and smarter, and you will be ready for something better when it comes along.

HOW MUCH OF YOUR FEAR OF FAILURE IS IRRATIONAL?

Are the people in your life *really* going to think less of you if you fail or are you just projecting your insecurities onto those around you? If some of them really would judge you for trying and failing, are they really people you want in your life? I certainly hope not. Now, if this person is someone who's with you for the long haul, like a family member or in-law, you need to think about ways to protect yourself from their negativity and criticism. Try setting boundaries by limiting the access they have to you and the information you give them.

HAVE YOU FAILED IN THE PAST? DID YOU SURVIVE?

As much as we find the idea of failure impossible to stomach, the reality is we have all failed before—and we're still here. You *will* survive it. Often on the show I will make the contestants tell me how they've failed and survived it in the past. I get them to see that they've *already* been to hell and back, and then I force them to call upon the resilience they've already built. If you survived in the past, you'll survive again—only this time you'll know how to swing failure to your advantage.

Another reason we fall into the vortex of the comfortably numb is to avoid pain and suffering, so that's the point we're hitting next.

BREAK THROUGH THE PAIN

> "The world breaks everyone, and afterward, some are stronger at the broken places."
>
> —ERNEST HEMINGWAY

Much like failure, pain is something we spend a lot of time and energy avoiding. If we shelter ourselves enough, we think we'll get through life with no pain. Unfortunately, this isn't reality. Pain and suffering exist for a reason, and running away does us more harm than good. You will never realize your full potential through an avoidance of pain. You can fight it—we all try to do so. But when you're exhausted, worn down, and realize that your efforts have been in vain, your best bet is to surrender, lean into it, and let it flow through you. It will leave you wiser and stronger in the end. The only true way out of pain is through it (as in the children's song: you can't go over it, you can't go under it, you have to go through it).

> "If you're going through hell, keep going."
>
> —WINSTON CHURCHILL

On *Biggest Loser* season six, we had an amazing contestant named Michelle. She came to the show full of piss and vinegar, determined to go all the way. By week three she was shattered: facing all the emotional pain that had gotten her to 242 pounds and estrangement from her mother seemed unbearable to her. By week five she had had enough and was ready to quit. Usually when someone I'm working with wants to walk out on their health, I let them. I can't want health for them. All I'm there to do is to give them the tools and to tell them how to use them—they have to do the work, and if they don't want to, then it's not going to happen.

But with Michelle it was different. I couldn't let her quit because it was working. Her pain was evidence that she was in the first stage of awareness. So I told her that she could quit the show and go home, but she would never move forward in her life until she processed whatever was coming to the surface. So Michelle and I made a pact: I would provide a safe environment for her breakdown, and she would lean into it. If you caught that season of the show, you'll know she came through the storm and ultimately, on the other side of it, was a smarter, stronger woman. She became so empowered, in fact, that she went on to win the whole competition. She is now happily married and inspiring women all over the world to confront their demons and follow their passions. If she hadn't allowed herself to feel that pain, she never would have succeeded.

We spend so much time running from what's difficult and shutting off our emotions, scrambling to stay in our comfortably numb place. A multibillion-dollar industry is devoted to manufacturing medications that will stop our emotions for us. Are you feeling sad, mad, or anxious? Whatever it is, chances are there's a pill for it. Awesome. It's yet another reason I hate many drug companies.

Human beings have evolved over thousands of years to have emotions. They exist for a reason. Our emotions are like an internal GPS system, guiding us out of unhappy or unhealthy situations and toward what's right. Remember the hot-cold game from Step One? Your emotions tell you when you're on track and when you're off it. You "listen to your gut" and "follow your heart." When you shut that part of yourself down, when you put your personal TomTom in the glove compartment, it becomes impossible to navigate back to your true path.

Many people live beneath their true potential because the minute they have a feeling of discontent, they swallow it down with a little Prozac. Their need to move out of the unhappiness dissipates, and they successfully reenter the world of the comfortably numb.

In most cases, antidepressants and elaborate defense mechanisms don't bring happiness—they block it. They don't protect you; they destroy you. Being numb to life is being asleep to its richness and fullness. The only way to know love is to know vulnerability. The only way to know happiness is to know sadness. Your ability to feel one emotion enhances your ability to feel the other. Remember that Kahlil Gibran quote from Chapter 1? "Your joy is your sorrow unmasked. And the selfsame well from which your laughter rises was oftentimes filled with your tears."

So what's the alchemy that turns pain into wisdom and joy? It's pretty simple: awareness, honesty, and time. You must be aware of your feelings and honor them by not stifling them. You must bring meaning to your pain by finding the lesson it holds. And with time, both will allow you to "become stronger in the broken places." It seems impossible to imagine when we are in the grip of suffering, but my mother used to say to me, as her mother used to say to her, and maybe as your mother has said to you . . . *This too shall pass.*

And it really will. Do not shut down. Be present and stay open. Almost every major event in our lives, especially the struggles, has a hidden meaning, and this meaning will serve you more than any other, if you choose to let it. This is the way to turn tragedy into triumph.

If you get fired, see it as a sign that you were meant for something else. Improve your skills, and pursue something better. If you go through a bad breakup or fall out with a friend, work on the issues that can enhance or deepen your connection in other relationships. Our darkest hours, like our failures, can be our greatest teachers.

WHEN THE WORST HAS HAPPENED

What about the kind of pain and sadness that can't be reasoned with or rationalized, like the death of a loved one? These things happen, and they are truly devastating. All I can offer you is a technique that helps me sleep at night—it's called logotherapy. (Yes, it has its own name.) Logotherapy was the invention of Viktor Frankl, an Austrian neurologist and psychiatrist as well as a Holocaust survivor who created a philosophy to help him get through his time in a concentration camp. The basic principles are these:

- Life has meaning under all circumstances, even the most miserable ones.
- Our main motivation for living is our will to find meaning in life.
- We have freedom to find meaning in what we do and what we experience, or at least in the stand we take when faced with unchangeable suffering.

Some of you out there are probably good and pissed at me for suggesting that horrible events have some sort of value. Ultimately everyone deals with "unchangeable suffering" in their own way, and I'm not here to start a religion. But personally I believe that to make the best of my situation, I have to create meaning from it, both in the best of times and in the worst. And I figure that if someone could find meaning in something as incomprehensible and horrendous as a concentration camp, my struggles and losses are minor; they are nothing. Let me give you a few examples of how you can apply this technique. This first is from Frankl himself, and it concerns a man who had lost his soul mate.

Once, an elderly general practitioner consulted me because of his severe depression. He could not overcome the loss of his wife who had died two years before and whom he had loved above all else. Now how could I help him? What should I tell him? I refrained from telling him anything, but instead confronted him with a question. "What would have happened, Doctor, if you had died first, and your wife would have had to survive you?" "Oh," he said, "for her this would have been terrible; how she would have suffered!" Whereupon I replied, "You see, Doctor, such a suffering has been spared her, and it is you who have spared her this suffering; but now, you have to pay for it by surviving and mourning her." He said no word but shook my hand and calmly left the office.*

When I first read that story, I got chills and cried for about ten minutes straight. Sometimes we have no choice but to suffer and sacrifice, but we can give that suffering purpose by becoming a vessel for goodness in the world. I'm not suggesting you become a martyr. You *know* that's not my thing. But if something horrible happens to you and you have no control over it, altruism and a belief in the greater good might carry you through. Frankl's story about the doctor and his wife is sad, but it's not rooted in darkness or tragedy. A loss of that kind, although soul-crushing, is part of nature's plan and for that reason possibly easier to bear.

But what do we do with life's unimaginable tragedies—dark events like genocide or murder, based in malevolence and born of evil? (Yes, I do believe that evil exists. It's not inherent, but born from unmanaged tragedy.) How can such horrors be purposeful and result in goodness in any way? The reality is that if you were involved in these things, you would find meaning in them, and the likelihood is that your sanity would depend on your doing so.

Bear with me for one more example. This story of the human spirit at its most transformative has gotten me through many a dark hour. In 1981 a six-year-old named Adam Walsh was kidnapped from a Sears near his Florida home and was brutally

* Viktor Frankl, *Man's Search for Meaning* (Boston: Beacon Press, 1959).

murdered. The details of the murder were atrocious, the real-
ization of any parent's worst nightmare; the death of a child,
especially such a violent one, must be one of the hardest things
anyone can go through. But instead of letting the pain of the
loss crush him, John Walsh, Adam's father, did just the opposite. He became an advocate for victims of violent crimes and
eventually went on to create and host *America's Most Wanted*,
Fox's longest-running TV show. As of July 15, 2010, some 1,123
criminals had been captured worldwide due to his work.

Walsh brought meaning and purpose to a tragedy that was
unthinkable. He transmuted the darkness of his son's murder
into a vehicle to protect other innocent victims from devastation.
The show will never fully heal the pain, obviously. But "God"/
the universe doesn't give us anything we can't handle. In fact, I
believe that people are subjected to these kinds of struggles and
tragedies because they *are* strong enough to find the meaning in
the tragedy and to turn the suffering into love.

I love philosophy, and a lot of times when I can't sleep, I listen
to podcasts by philosophers on everything from infinity to wine.
In one lecture, about "the problem of evil," the speaker raised
the question of whether compassion could exist in the world
without evil. (Similarly, how would we feel deep happiness if we
didn't know sadness?) None of us want evil to enter our lives, but
we may have no choice in the matter—John Walsh and Viktor
Frankl didn't. But what they did afterward shows us the flip side:
that light can penetrate the darkness.

How can the evils or tragedies that may have befallen you provide an entry point for goodness? This is a *huge* question, and I
can't answer it for you. You'll have to take it with you and answer
it as you go about the work of living. *You* must bring the meaning.
All I can do is tell you it's there if you look for it. The application
of this philosophy isn't easy. No true victory ever is. But we are
programmed survivors, and you can get through *anything* if you
lean into it, learn from it, and transform it.

INSTANT KARMA

This last bit on attitude is going to be short and sweet, because it's *obvious*. When I say karma, I'm not talking about reincarnation. If you're into that, cool; if you're not, that's cool, too. What I'm talking about here is your basic "do unto others" stuff. Your karma is the total effect of your actions and conduct over the course of your life, and it determines the shape of your life. It embodies a lot of what we've been talking about in a nice neat little package. If you want to see it as psychology, remember that all relationships are nothing more than a mirror of your relationship with yourself. If you want to get spiritual, remember that we are magnetic beings who attract the things we focus on. However you want to see it, we get back what we do and think, especially when it comes to our treatment of others.

Karma works in both directions, good and bad. If you're shitty to people, then life will probably be shitty to you. If you're good to people, most likely good things will ultimately come back to you. You really do reap what you sow. Or if you want to get a little more highbrow, we can go with Gandhi, who said, "Be the change you want to see in the world." You make a choice about what you want to put out there.

I bet you're thinking, *I have seen total assholes become wildly successful, so how can this be true?* Well, so have I. But consider: you don't know the quality of their personal lives, health, or spiritual happiness. My father was a *very* successful man, and I'm sure to the outside world his life seemed perfect, but sadly, I don't believe he was or has ever been happy. Remember that old saying "You can't judge a book by its cover"? Know this: a happy, self-satisfied person does not feel the need to attack, belittle, or undervalue other human beings.

Often people aren't kind to others because they feel the world hasn't been kind to them. They are hurting and feel powerless, so they hurt others as a way to have power over those people, like a bully in the schoolyard. And don't we all know that the bullies are the most scared and insecure people?

I want you to take one thing away from this small section of the book: I want you to be one of the good guys, so that life will be good to you. Don't judge others, and don't be a "hater." By gossiping, labeling, and tearing people down, you waste precious time and energy, and you attract negativity. You're creating a black hole that will suck in you and everything in your life.

Did you ever play a game called King of the Hill when you were a kid? One player climbs to the top of the hill, and all the other players try to knock him off by pushing or pulling at him. Everyone gets bruised up and bashed around. Even the person at the top can't enjoy their stay there. Negativity blocks your ability to receive positive things. Stop wasting energy on fruitless endeavors of jealousy and envy. Isn't that one of the seven deadly sins? Quit coming from a place of fear and lacking. Remember that there is abundance in the universe. Invite its flow, and add some action to create the outcome you desire. Instead of fighting, build your own castle at the top of your own hill!

Let's look beyond the obvious reasons why we shouldn't be petty and hurtful. All the great spiritual and psychological teachers talk about our oneness, which is ultimately why the laws of karma exist in some form in every belief system. What you do to others, you do to yourself. One of my favorite theories on this subject is Carl Jung's notion of the collective unconscious. He thought this innate structure encompassed the universal thoughts of all humanity. If we could get deep enough into all of our minds, he believed, we'd get to a level of knowledge that we all share. It was a sort of "reservoir of the experiences of our species" made up of concepts like science, morality, and religion. He then got really out there and suggested that at an even deeper level, we all have the same mind. At our core, we're not just identical, we're the same being.

It's heavy, I know. But in a way it's comforting, and in my heart I believe it. We are all made up of the same matter and energy—we just express it differently. I like to think of people as stained-glass windows: we're all different and unique in our designs, colors, and themes, but the light that shines through your window is the same light that shines through mine. And even though the window can shatter, the energy that illuminates it is eternal.

I'm giving you a lot to chew on, but the bottom line is, you've got to do unto others as you would have them do unto you. Be open, accepting, and giving whenever possible, within your own healthy boundaries. When you are willing to give away the very thing you're in search of, you keep abundance in circulation in all our lives. If it is money you want, be generous. If it's love and support, be loving and encouraging toward others. Whatever it is you want, if you generate it and get it out there, it will come back to you.

CHAPTER EIGHT

STOP SELLING YOURSELF SHORT

This is the big one, the topic that everything else in Step Two has been leading up to. The premise of this book is that anyone can achieve anything. The only *if* in the equation is your belief in yourself. Do you believe you are capable of doing the work necessary to go after the life you want? Just as important, do you believe you're worth it?

Every single person I've ever helped has had one thing in common with all the others: initially they had zero self-esteem. It's no wonder they were lost. Self-esteem is a person's overall evaluation of his or her worth. If you feel worthless, then buddy, join a big club. Many, many people struggle with esteem issues.

In Step One I told you how to conceptualize, crystallize, and attach yourself to a vision for the life of your dreams. And in Step Three, I'm going to lead you through the process of taking deliberate, powerful action to bring that vision into reality. Step Two is the hardest part of this whole formula, but it's also the linchpin.

Learning to believe in yourself is the most important step you will ever take toward unleashing your inner power. I can give you a step-by-step success action plan, whether it's on how to lose weight, how to find the love of your life, or how to find the perfect job. Horse, meet water. But if you lack the self-esteem to follow it, then it doesn't matter what powerful information is imparted to you—you will still be lost (and thirsty).

Low self-esteem is the poison that erodes the connection between your actions and your intentions. Believing in yourself is an essential part of healthy functioning in all aspects of your life.

People with positive self-esteem have healthier, stronger connections to others. They know how to set boundaries and express needs, and they value their own contributions to a mutually appreciated partnership. Once in high school, when I was struggling with some jerk boyfriend, my dad said to me, "Boys will treat you as badly as you let them." (My father from time to time could impart good advice. Like I told you, people are not black-and-white.) He was right, and it's not just a man-woman thing, it's a *people* thing. If you value yourself and treat yourself with respect, you will be valued and respected. If you don't, you won't. It's really that simple. Even if someone does value and respect you in spite of your self-deprecating ways, you won't have the self-esteem to believe in their feelings for you, and you won't accept them at face value, so the relationship won't be able to flourish.

Self-esteem is the key to success in any endeavor, from work to weight loss. Without it our self-destructive patterns corrode our love lives, careers, family bonds, and most important, our internal sense of well-being and strength. We can't take the risks or make the decisions necessary to lead fulfilling, productive lives. We don't feel worthy or capable, and as a result we shy away from life rather than engaging in it, too afraid that we aren't equipped to handle the challenges of a fully lived life. Even if you manage to overcome a setback or reach a goal, without a foundation of truly valuing yourself, you run the risk of sabotaging your success.

This is one of the top reasons that people backslide after they've achieved a goal. They don't feel they deserve the happiness their success will bring them, so they destroy what they've accomplished. Or they start down the path to happiness but quit before the finish, afraid that once they show the world they can do something, the world will have a new set of expectations. Now that they've proved they're able, the world will expect success of them, and they can no longer fall back on a lack of aptitude. They worry about their ability to continue succeeding; as with success, the risk of letting people down is exponentially higher. And to people with low self-esteem, disappointing others is the worst thing imaginable, because they define their own value by pleasing others. How many of you are guilty of this pattern?

When I was a kid, I was the Olympic gold medalist in this game. I would set my mind on something, work my ass off till success was in sight, and then walk away. I was deeply afraid that if I got to the end and failed, I would be a massive disappointment. My parents, friends, and teachers would see that I was incompetent, and why would anyone want to be around a loser? How could my parents be proud of me? Why would my teachers waste time with me? Blah, blah, blah. You already know the words to this song.

I always found a way to justify quitting before the finish. *That's good enough. I don't need to see it through to the end.* Or *Now I've gotten this far, it would be a waste of time to finish it.* Or *I'm bored with this now and I want to learn something else. Interesting people are always moving on and learning new things.* It wasn't till I was twenty that someone showed me how to break this pattern.

From the time I was twelve, I studied martial arts. (Yes, I know you know that by now.) In martial arts I found a place to be strong and healthy, and it felt good. Over the course of five years, I went from a white belt to a third-degree red belt (which for us was right before black), and then at seventeen I quit. I'd developed a real bond with my instructor, and it drove him crazy that I just walked away. Poor guy. For the next three years he would ask me to come back, to "finish what you started."

But my self-esteem was still fragile from my past, and I was so well defended against the possibility of happiness and success that I shut him out. If I had actually finished the process and earned the black belt, I would have had to let go of the fat loser kid I still felt like. Who would I be then? What would I have to fall back on? Who would this new, successful Jillian be? What if she ended up being a disappointment? She would have no excuses—and no reasons to justify "I can't." I was terrified. I didn't return his calls or his letters. I even pretended I'd moved! Seriously, I started stamping his letters "Return to Sender." One day, just before my twenty-first birthday, he wrote me one last letter. For some reason, I chose to open it. This is what I read:

> Jillian,
>
> It's been a while now. I understand that you are scared and fearful of success and failure, whether you admit it or not.
>
> It's very hard for me to develop a close bond with a student and push them away. However, this will be my last attempt to persuade you. Ultimately your decisions in life must be your own. I now know how a mother bird must feel when she shoves the chick from the nest to fall or fly.
>
> The black belt test is the pinnacle of our journey together. After the black belt test I accomplish what I set out to do when I first started teaching. The student becomes his or her own hero, steps out from under the teacher's protective shadow, and becomes a master. A special, powerful person who looks to themselves first.
>
> As I have said before . . . you were 95% of the way there. If we had three more months we could have completed that process.
>
> You have had some major conflicts and survived. You landed on your own two feet and learned to depend on yourself. Remember that feeling and trust it now. It's time for you to become your own master. The creator of your own destiny. The hero you are meant to be.
>
> I want you to know that I am proud of who you are and what you have already accomplished. I think you are an incredible young woman, and we have done a hell of a lot together. My heart and my home are ALWAYS open to you, and when you are

*ready, please, come back and finish your training. I'd like to see
a black belt around your waist.*

*Good luck in all you do. It's 4:30am. Time to go swing my
sword in the hills and howl at the moon with the coyotes.*

Take care,

Sensei

(I know what you're thinking. Yes, he really did write that bit
about the sword and the moon. So he's a little eccentric. Some of
the best of us are!)

This letter spoke to me loud and clear. From the moment I read
it, I knew I had to become my own person, to step up and face life
full on. It was time for me to let go of the fat loser kid once and
for all. I went back to the dojo, trained for a year, and got my black
belt in Akarui-do (the way of the light). It was a turning point in
my life, the beginning of everything.

I still had a long way to go, but I had *done* something. And I
hadn't done it for anyone else. Sure, the cheers and pats on the
back were great. But I'd done it for myself, and that was what
felt the best. I nurtured this feeling of accomplishment and car-
ried it with me like armor. I applied it to every task or situation
I approached, allowing it to give me that quiet inner strength it
takes to go after what you want. Even now I'll catch myself thinking, "If I finished my black belt training, I can do anything!"

This is another reason I beat the crap out of the *Biggest Loser*
contestants the way I do. I know that when they go back home
and are forced to face all their painful demons, they will be able
to rely on the inner strength they built from the grueling hours
of punishment I dished out in the gym. They have point-blank
said to me, "After living through several months with you, Jillian
Michaels, there is nothing I can't endure."

Problems with self-esteem are particularly insidious because
like many other emotional issues, they often begin in childhood.
So by the time we're adults, we think it's normal to doubt ourselves

at every turn, to lose ourselves in any relationship we enter into, and to sit life out because of fear of the unknown.

I always found the term *dysfunctional family* to be somewhat amusing, because it implies that *functional* is the norm, but most families operate with at least a little dysfunction in the mix. Of course it's all relative, and some of us come into adulthood with a lot more baggage than others. (Think back to Shay in Chapter 5—that's dysfunction taken to its most dreadful extreme.) But we all have varying levels of dysfunction in our family backgrounds and relationships—it's just the nature of the beast. I believe our life's mission is to work through these issues in order to grow and adapt. The key words here: *working through the issues*. When you don't, they have the potential to greatly inhibit and even destroy the joy and purpose of your life.

Remember the story of the chained elephants? If you have grown up believing that you're not good enough, how are you going to know any different when it comes time for you to go out into the world? I believe who you become as a person is a mix of nature and nurture, but even someone with the best biochemistry and the strongest, clearest mind can be conditioned into believing they lack value and don't deserve success or happiness.

Here's another story from the show. One of my Australian *Biggest Loser* contestants was a wonderful guy with boatloads of potential. During the first few weeks he was on campus, he was busting all the past seasons' weight-loss records. He worked hard. He was likable. And week after week that weight kept coming off. But then I found out something that set off some major alarm bells: he'd been to similar weight-loss camps, and each time he'd lost a huge amount of weight—only to gain it all back, and then some.

What was going to keep it from happening again?

I took him aside and put some tough questions to him. What had been happening in his life when he lost the weight before? What had been happening when he put it back on? How many years had this cycle been going on? Did any pivotal events coincide with his original weight gain? I grilled him and wouldn't let him get away with half-assed answers.

If you watch the show, I'm sure you've seen me do this before. Without fail, the contestants reach for easy, noncommittal answers: "I don't know" or "I can't remember." But those aren't answers! Those are the self-defense mechanisms that we all use to shield ourselves from unpleasant truths. Sometimes we need to dig out the unpleasant truths in order to liberate ourselves from whatever is holding us back. Once you start digging, you'll find the answers are right there, waiting for you to unearth them.

So back to my contestant. I kept up the third degree with him until he was at the point of mental and emotional exhaustion. It was kind of like an interrogation scene from a spy movie, only without the torture. (Contrary to what some people might think, I do draw the line somewhere!) Finally the answers came pouring out of him, and the sad secrets of his past saw the light of day for the first time in fifteen years.

It turned out that he had had an older sibling who became ill and died when he was in his late teens. That was when his weight gain started. His parents had shuffled him from one relative to another while trying to take care of their sick child. While they were doing the best they could under unbearable circumstances, my poor contestant felt that his whole world had vanished—all of a sudden, not only was his sibling suffering from a life-threatening illness, but he had lost the security of being home with his parents. That and the actual death was a lot of loss for anyone to deal with, let alone a fourteen-year-old kid.

When we experience such loss, sadness isn't the only emotion we feel. This contestant also struggled inwardly with anger—at God for letting this happen to his brother, at his brother for dying, at his parents for abandoning him. Then came shame—shame that he was angry. He must be a horrible person to feel angry—after all, he wasn't the one who'd lost his life. He also felt guilt and shame that he had lived. And that shame was the root of his self-loathing.

To cope with all his feelings—loneliness, guilt, sadness, anger—he began compulsively overeating. That of course only added to the burden of shame he was carrying around. Sure he'd try to get healthy, but whenever he'd get close to his ideal weight, he'd self-sabotage, because deep down he still felt he had to atone for being a bad person, for living, and so on. Needless to say, the longer this went on, the deeper the original feelings of anger and shame got buried, and the worse the cycle became.

Pretty heavy, right? But the thing is, once he really looked at where his struggles with weight originated, he was able to take the necessary steps to heal and move on. No longer at the mercy of his stifled emotions, he was able to recognize the triggers of his unhealthy habits and sabotaging behaviors. He went back and grieved his original hurt without feeling ashamed. He came to learn that his feelings were justified and need not be buried. This allowed him to work through those feelings and release them, then begin to build up his self-esteem from there. He was no longer putting a minefield between himself and his health.

Self-esteem is a self-fulfilling prophecy: the more you like yourself, the more you begin to act in likable ways. The more you believe you are able to achieve something, the more likely you are to do so. "You achieve what you believe." You know I love a cliché. Self-esteem gives you the power to exude the confidence, ability, and assertiveness you need to drive yourself toward your full potential and toward physical and emotional well-being.

So what do you do if you have buried, diminished, or misplaced your self-esteem? Fortunately, there are steps you can take to build and strengthen it. Before we begin, let's take inventory of your self-esteem today. I've put together a little quiz that will help you figure out where you fall on the scale of self-loathing to self-love, and assess how much you're undercutting yourself with guilt, shame, anger, and self-deprecation. Your answers will shed light on the issues that need working on, to better focus your restorative energy. Let's do it!

From Self-Loathing to Self-Love

1. **Most of the time I am:**
   a) Happy or content
   b) Sad and angry
   c) Numb and depressed

2. **Whether I am celebrating a success or comforting myself after a bad day, I reward myself with a self-destructive behavior like bingeing, compulsive spending, or drinking too much:**
   a) Rarely
   b) Frequently
   c) All the time

3. **I am able to communicate my needs to my family, friends, and coworkers:**
   a) All the time
   b) Frequently
   c) Rarely

4. **When I make a mistake:**
   a) I allow myself to feel disappointed, then learn from it so I can reapproach the problem and solve it.
   b) I am furious with myself and will make sure I win next time.
   c) I am devastated and fear trying again.

5. **I care what others think:**
   a) Hardly ever
   b) Frequently
   c) All the time

6. **I hate to look in the mirror:**
   a) Rarely
   b) Frequently
   c) All the time

7. I have trouble asking others for help:
   a) Rarely
   b) Frequently
   c) All the time

8. I speak negatively about myself—call myself fat, stupid, lazy, etc.:
   a) Rarely
   b) Frequently
   c) All the time

QUIZ
Where Do
You Fall?

9. I do nice things for myself:
   a) All the time
   b) Frequently
   c) Rarely

10. I apologize:
   a) Only when the problem is directly my fault
   b) Frequently, even if the issue isn't directly my fault
   c) All the time. Even if I just bump into someone by accident, I say "sorry" instead of "excuse me."

11. If my food is not prepared well, or if the order is wrong at a restaurant:
   a) I send it right back.
   b) I apologize to the waiter and ask if they wouldn't mind fixing it.
   c) I say nothing and eat it anyway.

12. When people ask me to do things, and I don't want to do them or don't have time, I do them anyway because I don't want to disappoint people and prefer to put everyone else's needs before my own. (Examples: doing carpool for the neighbor, picking up your uncle from the airport, volunteering at your nephew's school— all in the same week, sometimes the same day.)

    a) Rarely

    b) Frequently

    c) All the time

13. **I went on a job interview, but I didn't get the job, so:**
    a) I asked the interviewer for feedback, analyzed where I could improve my answers or interview style, trusted that everything happens for a reason, and knew that there would be other opportunities.
    b) I knew I wasn't smart enough for that job. It was out of my league, and I shouldn't have applied for it.
    c) I panicked and feared that I would never work again.

14. **When I am complimented:**
    a) I accept the compliment and say thank you.
    b) I get uncomfortable.
    c) I negate the compliment.

15. **I am comfortable expressing my angry or sad feelings:**
    a) All the time
    b) Frequently
    c) Rarely

16. **I actively pursue relationships with people I like:**
    a) All the time
    b) Frequently
    c) Rarely

17. **When a friend or acquaintance gets a promotion or falls in love, I feel:**
    a) Thrilled for them and inspired by their happiness
    b) A little envious, but I know my time will come
    c) Sick with jealousy

SCORE: Add up as follows: (a)=1, (b)=2, (c)=3

RESULTS

17–21 AWESOME: Wow! Really? Good for you! You have a very strong sense of who you are and your value in this world, and you don't live small for anyone. You respect yourself and aren't jealous or envious of those around you. You are secure about asking for help because you know you are worth it and that you will one day pay it forward. You lead a balanced, happy life, and when the opportunity arises to grow and improve yourself, you're always ready.

22–29 PRETTY GOOD: You're doing better than most. You know who you are and what you're about. For the most part you feel deserving, and more often than not you put pursuit of happiness at the top of the list. You can get stuck in a rut, but you work hard to dig your way out of it. You are secure enough to work on yourself and will lean on friends and family when you absolutely have to, because you know that when their time of need comes, you can also be supportive.

30–40 NOT SUPER: You aren't a total mess, but you sure have room for a little healthy ego strengthening. You can be critical and unforgiving of yourself. You find your value by facilitating other people's happiness and often put their needs before your own. You are quick to take the blame when things go wrong, and you tend to get in your own way by not allowing yourself room for mistakes or time to learn from them.

41–51 REALLY CRAPPY: My heart is breaking for you. Feel that? It's me coming through the pages and giving you a giant hug. You have no sense of self-worth. You allow the whims of others to define you. You rarely do anything for yourself, and your whole identity is about pleasing others, no matter how much of yourself you have to repress to do it. You beat yourself up and pick yourself apart at every opportunity. This is a horrible way to exist. I hope you are really paying attention to this book, 'cuz buddy, you need it.

———

Do *not* be bummed if you did poorly. This test isn't designed to judge you. Its only purpose is to make you aware of your current state, to get you thinking and ready to focus on living your best life. And hey, even if you did as badly on the quiz as it's possible to do, if you bought this book, it means that you recognize something is off and you're already taking steps to change it.

Okay, now that we have established where your heart and your head are, we're ready to get going with some simple methods to help you build, nurture, and fortify your sense of self-worth. On the following pages I've outlined some basic thought exercises and have even included some activities you can do to help get you started. As you can see from the quiz results, even if you did great, we all have issues that we can work on and areas of our self-esteem that could do with a little bolstering.

This will not come easily or quickly. Unfortunately, self-esteem doesn't come in pill form—*you* have to build it for yourself, and it is going to take some hard and solitary work on your part. It's sort of like a workout regimen for your spirit—it'll take some time, and no one else but you can do it. Of course it helps a hell of a lot to have loving, supportive people in your life cheering you on and telling you you're awesome, but at the end of the day the onus of connecting to and nurturing your inner value falls on you and you alone.

I can tell you that you are unlimited until the cows come home (what does that mean, anyway?), but it only matters if *you* believe it. It *will* come if you are diligent.

Don't be put off by the effort involved. Is there anything more important than your relationship with yourself? I don't think so. After all, it's the one thing you can control and it controls all you do.

One last thing: I want to tell you to be prepared for some ups and downs.

Like the pursuit of any worthwhile goal, you may find that you backslide—don't beat yourself up. You know the five-steps-forward, three-steps-back drill. Remember that success is largely a matter of attrition, of just "showing up" (thank you, Woody Allen). So be patient and loving with yourself, and keep showing up. Even if you don't feel that what you're doing is having an effect, it is. Have a little faith—I know what I'm talking about.

Ready?

TAKE STOCK OF YOUR ACCOMPLISHMENTS

It's time to start a list. I want you to write down some of the successes that you have achieved in any and every area of your life. These achievements do not have to be life-changing, earth-shattering moments of crowning glory. They can be tiny, anything from accomplishing a good hair day to making a well-cooked breakfast! (I'm not kidding—I made eggs over easy the other morning without breaking the yoke, and I was slapping myself on the back all day. It's the little things. . . .) There's always *something* you can feel good about and be proud of having done. Did you finally clean out your closets and get those old clothes to the Salvation Army? Did you pay your taxes on time? Did you cook a great dinner for friends or family the other night? Then write it down! There's no time limit—keep adding to it as you go about your daily life. In this way, you will create a list of successes that you can refer to in times of fear and self-doubt.

Whenever you are feeling afraid or defeated, take out the list—whether it's recorded on a piece of paper or on your iPhone—and go over it, reinforcing the feelings of competence and strength that come with achieving anything, great or small. When we take note of our achievements, we learn through personal, hands-on experience that we actually *are* capable. By creating an emotional atmosphere that amplifies your self-worth in this way, you can begin to believe in your abilities to achieve even more.

CREATE A SMALL VICTORY

While the first exercise focuses on successes you have already achieved, this exercise will focus on going out and creating more. Our experiences, whether recent or long past, help us define who we are and what we are capable of. If our life is one where the glass has been half empty, then failure and disillusionment become self-fulfilling prophecies. Now we're going to use the same trick of the mind to program you for success. The very same thought patterns that have eroded your belief in yourself can also build it back up.

Let's go back and take another look at Shay from Chapter 5. It's week one. She is in the gym with Bob and me for the first time. In a matter of days, she could be eliminated from the show and sent packing, back home to keep committing suicide by food. The clock is ticking. Now, Shay is not stupid. She knows that diet and exercise are her keys to weight loss and health—lack of knowledge is *not* one of her issues. Her problem is much simpler and much more heartbreaking, not to mention much more universal: she doesn't feel capable of the work or worthy of the end result.

I know that the *only* way to change that is to create new experiences for her, experiences where she proves to herself that she is capable of strength and success. It doesn't have to be a huge triumph—it's not like I'm going to tell her to run a marathon. Any little achievement will do. We then take that achievement, plant it like a seed, nourish it with appreciation, and watch it grow.

So it's do or die in the gym, literally. I'm trying to get Shay to climb the rotating ladder for thirty more seconds, and she's totally falling apart. Crying, sliding off the equipment, making all kinds of negative statements: "I can't do this!" "I'm in too much pain!" "I just want to go home!" She's working overtime, but at the exact wrong thing—she's trying desperately to write the same old story that she's a failure who's destined for misery. With all the patience I can muster (and you know that's not my strong suit) I spend a half hour trying to coax her back onto the ladder to do a full thirty-second climb. I'm sweet. I'm kind. I'm loving. Nothing gets through to her. But if she doesn't climb the ladder, she will see it as one more piece of evidence that she is incapable, further proof that she is a lost cause.

· If you saw episode one of season eight, you may remember what happened next. I unleashed. I wasn't going to let Shay continue telling herself she "couldn't" ANYTHING. She wasn't going to continue gathering evidence of her ineptitude, not on my watch. I screamed and cursed at the top of my lungs: "Shay get on the fucking ladder!!! GET ON THE FUCKING LADDER NOW, SHAY!!!" It was not pretty. I grabbed her by the shirt and literally threw/pushed/pulled her onto the ladder and continued screaming bloody murder at her to climb or else.

And you know what? In those few moments, Shay was so terrified of me that her fear circumvented her internal dialogue of "I can't." She was too afraid of *me* to remember to tell herself that she couldn't do it, and so she did it. And not just one thirty-second climb either—she ended up doing five that day, and the day after that she did five consecutive minutes. After that she stopped telling herself "I can't," and she went on to break the record for the fastest hundred-pound weight loss by a woman contestant.

Don't get me wrong—I'm not suggesting you need to be verbally assaulted, or that a maniac has to threaten to rip your arms off and beat you with them, if you are to escape the negative inner monologue that keeps you down. It's really up to you to get yourself out of your comfort zone, read from a new script, and give yourself a chance at the life you deserve. As your confidence builds, slowly you'll begin to realize that the whole notion that you are incapable is utter crap.

How quickly this happens varies from person to person. Some people need to make many little achievements before they snap out of it and realize that they're actually competent, effective human beings. For others, the "aha" moment is practically instantaneous; they realize with the first success, even if it's tiny, that everything damning that they have thought about themselves is untrue. The prison in which they have been living is a construct of their imagination, and they're free to toss those shackles off and fly. Please don't think I mean that only success will follow—you *will* have setbacks, trials, failures. But as you slowly build your self-esteem, your self-image will be redefined. You will see yourself as a person who learns from mistakes and overcomes adversity, rather than a person who gets devastated by them.

It's important, especially at first, that you are measured in your risk-taking. When I was screaming at Shay, it was over *thirty seconds* on a workout ladder—something *anyone* with two functioning legs should be capable of doing. It's important that the risk I wanted her to take was something I *knew* she could do. Setting her up for failure would have been the worst thing at that moment.

It's the same for you. You have to be smart about what you decide to go for and pick something that's achievable. For example, if you haven't jogged in five years, don't get out there and try to run a mile. Instead, go out and jog for 60 seconds, then walk for 60 seconds to recover; do this for 20 to 30 minutes. Then build on that in baby steps. The next week go for 90-second jogs. Then 120 seconds, and so on. If you can do more than that and advance faster, awesome, but the key is to make sure you give yourself something achievable to do, so you can build your self-confidence.

Success begets success. Once you start really focusing on the sense of accomplishment you get from achieving a result, even a minor one, it will help you to shut down negative emotions like anxiety and self-doubt, and you'll find yourself up for bigger and bigger challenges. Before you know it, your baby steps have become huge strides forward.

RELEASE GUILT AND SHAME

As long as you are carrying guilt and shame around with you, you will never be able to build a healthy sense of self. These emotions really only serve to indicate that you have taken on someone else's crap, or that you haven't taken proper steps to right a wrong you inflicted. Beyond that, all they do is waste your energy and make you feel bad. Who needs that?

This is the same stuff we talked about in Chapter 5, on forgiveness and understanding, but I bring it up again here because recognizing how you have taken on other people's fears, anxieties, and issues is a crucial step on the road to taking your life back. What do you feel guilty or ashamed about? Usually it is nothing more than a trip someone else has laid on you that you have internalized. By recognizing that other people have shortcomings and issues, too, we avoid making them our own, leaving us to travel light, without the baggage of those around us.

Not buying it? Positive that your guilt and shame belong to you? It's possible, but unlikely, so let's go in for a closer look. Guilt is when you feel bad about something you have done, as in *I bought myself a flat-screen TV and now I feel guilty because that was so selfish and indulgent of me.* Is treating yourself really something you should be feeling guilty about? The actual *reasons* you feel guilty are usually that someone has told you or implied that what you have done is bad. Suppose you take this scenario to its worst case: you have a compulsive spending problem, you're strapped for cash, *and* you didn't ask your significant other before making the purchase. You *still* shouldn't feel guilty, because it's unproductive. It will only further erode your self-esteem, making your issues that much worse. The answer is to work on your spending problem and to make amends with your spouse or partner.

Shame can get confused with guilt because they often go hand in hand, but they are different. Shame is the humiliation and embarrassment that can come as a result of guilt, but it doesn't always have to stem from something we have done. Some of us experience shame for just literally being.

I have known people who were raised to be ashamed of their physicality, ethnicity, religion, sexual orientation, the town they were born in, and so on. Now I ask you, as a sane good-hearted person, where is the shame in any of those things? No matter who you are, what your background is, or where you come from, you have *nothing* to be ashamed of. Shame is a feeling that is put upon us both directly and indirectly. No child is born ashamed of themselves—it's ingrained over time. "You oughta be ashamed of yourself"—remember that one? Or it could be as simple as pick- ing up on something your family and friends felt uncomfortable about and then internalizing it and making it about you. Sort of like kids can do with a divorce. The parents are unhappy, so they split up, but the kid might take it on and believe that it was his fault. If only he were a better kid, they would have been happy and stayed together. And the shame of feeling like a failure or a disap- pointment sets in—even though the divorce had nothing to do with him, and the parents had actually hated each other for years and finally got healthy enough to end the unhealthy relationship.

Anyone who is directly manipulating, judging, and/or sham- ing you is a person with his or her own issues. They can play on your emotions to get you to do something they want. Ever been guilted by your parents about visiting them for Christmas when you really need a vacation to the Bahamas? Now, whether you choose to go home for Christmas is up to you. Go or don't go, but there's no need to place all this emotional baggage on the situation. It's up to you to opt to take that on or not. You have a choice!

Another possibility is that someone is projecting the things in his life that he is afraid of or feels insecure about onto you. Often we fear things that are different because we don't understand them, and that's scary, or it challenges our dearly held beliefs and way of life, which can be even scarier. For that reason we can resent those things and condemn others for being so different.

More people have died due to fighting over religious beliefs than any other known cause of death.

When it comes to shame, ask yourself if the things you feel ashamed about are truly unnatural and deplorable. I highly doubt they are! Most likely you picked up these judgments and shameful feelings along the way, whether from our culture or our families and such.

Let me give you another example of the way we pick up shame *indirectly*. Let's say you are overweight and you feel that it's "gross." You hate your body. You won't work out in a gym with thin people because you're afraid of what they'll think of you. I have heard women say they are humiliated for their husbands to see them naked. That's so sad. Where did this attitude come from? Fat is merely stored energy. It is a physical state, nothing more and nothing less. It implies zero about your value as a person in this world. In fact, some cultures glorify being heavy and consider it a sign of affluence. Now, I am not suggesting it's okay for you to let your health go. (It's not! Your family and friends want you around for years to come.) But I'm trying to point out that the opinions we form about ourselves are taken on, not intrinsic.

So where did your shameful attitudes come from? Did you pick them up like a common cold? Actually, yeah, sort of. We are social creatures, and we are inclined to pick up the ideals, energies, and attitudes of those around us. Maybe your parents made an issue of your weight as a kid, asked you in front of friends, "Do you really want to eat that?" Or possibly they weighed you every week, making you subconsciously feel that if you didn't hit the benchmark, you would be unlovable and so on. In most cases this is not malicious on the parents' part. It's usually just misguided concern: concern that they should be doing something, and helpless because they don't know what. They also probably worried that people would believe they didn't care about their kid's health if you were overweight, and so they overcompensated by nagging and pestering every time you put anything in your mouth. But even though the comments clearly stem from your parents' insecurities, of course you're going to feel you need fixing. Thus the shame of "not being good enough" or letting your parents down sets in.

Maybe your shameful attitude has nothing to do with your parents. Maybe you feel ashamed of your weight because on the schoolyard as a kid your peers tormented you by making cow noises when they walked behind you. (This one comes from my own personal junior high hell.) Still, kids who bully on the playground are kids who feel insecure and powerless, so they pick on others in an attempt to have power over someone else and regain a feeling of control. Yep, we already covered that ground, so I hope you are starting to see the pattern.

Your feelings of shame were originally someone else's—you picked up on them and internalized them. The simple fact is that obesity can be caused by many things, like lack of knowledge, resources, and finances. It can be an emotional coping mechanism. But none of those issues are gross or unnatural, or even unusual. Quite the contrary, they are painfully human, and overweight people deserve the proper love, care, and attention to improve. Shame is the absolute worst emotion one can bring to this situation, or any other for that matter.

This next anecdote is a more blatant example of one community's issues becoming another person's shame. I met a young boy once who was so ashamed of being gay that he would literally cry himself to sleep every night. His parents, friends, and community were passionately antigay, and this poor kid was devastated, humiliated, and filled with self-loathing. Now, had he not grown up being told that homosexuality was "evil and the work of the devil," he probably would have gone his whole life not thinking a thing of it. After all, he was born that way. It was his natural state, but most of the people in his life were afraid of homosexuality because it was different. They were taught that it was evil and threatened their way of life. This issue was theirs, not his, but because he was young and didn't have the ability to discern the distinction at that point in his life, he took on their baggage and all the shame, fear, and sadness that came with it.

It was only after I worked with this kid on his self-esteem for months and showed him examples of positive, healthy, happy gay men who are sources of strength and inspiration in the world that he shed the shame put upon him and was able to embrace the possibility of a bright future.

Shame is a dark emotion. I believe in my heart that everything has a purpose—except shame. Nothing—and I do mean nothing—good can come of it. Even if you did something that you feel ashamed about, shame is insidious and pointless and it's *still* indirectly a result of taking on someone else's shit. Think about it. If you tell or show a kid he's worthless, eventually he will believe it and subsequently he will act like it. Remember what I told you about Hitler and Saddam. Yes, extreme examples, but proof of my point.

While you may feel bad or guilty about something you may have done wrong, shame is not the solution. And guilt, like shame, is often an emotion we are conditioned to feel. Next time you are feeling guilty about something, stop to ask yourself if you actually did anything mean-spirited or malevolent.

When I was a kid, my dad used to tell me constantly that I was a spoiled and ungrateful brat. This was on a daily basis. For years, and even sometimes now, I was unable to accept anything from anyone. I couldn't even let friends buy me coffee without feeling guilty that I had "taken advantage" of them. Only a greedy person who couldn't or wouldn't take care of themselves would let others pay for them. I should be as fully self-sufficient as he was. After *years* of therapy, though, I understand that my dad called me a brat because of his own insecurities. It's clear to me now that he had horribly low self-esteem and felt he had nothing to offer those around him but money—which turned into a fear that people *only* spent time with him *because* of his money. He then projected those insecurities onto me, accusing me of loving him only when he gave me things.

Kids often don't have defenses against these kinds of criticisms, so for the longest time I thought that to want or accept something from someone was the worst thing in the world. But with time and self-awareness (and as I said, a *lot* of therapy), I was able to realize that part of being alive on this planet is give *and* take. Sometimes we need to accept generosity in order to pass that generosity on in some other form. I now understand where my dad's issues end and mine begin. And I was able to forgive him and move on to my bigger picture, getting healthy and whole so I could help other people get healthy and whole.

If in fact you have a real reason to feel guilty about something—you hurt someone, screwed something up, what have you—feelings of guilt *still* aren't going to get you anywhere. They're utterly destructive and only make things worse. Human beings make mistakes, sometimes horrible ones, but the only way to handle them is to learn from them, make amends, and make changes. Period.

> **"Whoever has done harmful actions but later covers them up with good is like the moon which, freed from clouds, lights up the world."**
> —THE BUDDHA

WORKING IT OUT

Let's put all this advice into practice and work on some exercises to release shame and guilt. *Forever.* This might make your skin crawl a bit. It will require revisiting some dark moments and getting close to some scary feelings of hurt, inadequacy, and humiliation—you may want to curl up in a ball just thinking about it. But it's important to pull these things out by the root. Once you do, you'll clear the way for a new, strong, loving sense of self-worth that no one will be able to destroy. Just say no to guilt and shame.

1. Start a "Shame and Blame" list. Not so that you can dwell on it and feel even worse about yourself, but so that you can identify

where other people have piled their crap onto yours and where you have piled your crap onto others. For each item on the list, ask yourself the following questions:

a) Was this my fault? If so, how can I take responsibility for it, make amends, and fix it?

b) If it wasn't my fault, whose issue is it really? Am I taking on someone else's stuff or trying to keep someone else from being angry, upset, or disappointed?

c) What do I contribute to making the issue worse? Do I beat myself up over it? Speak negatively about myself? Deprive myself of love and nurturing?

d) If I could get rid of my feelings of guilt or shame, what would the issue look like and how would it affect my life?

2. Make amends. If you have actually done something hurtful to someone else that you feel guilt and shame about, there is a way forward: making amends. This will not be a comfortable task, but it's the only path to your emotional freedom. You go to the other person and accept responsibility for the part you played. Offer a sincere apology. Vow to change your behavior and never to make the same mistake. (Talk is cheap. Action is what counts most. "Sorry" alone doesn't cut it.) And last, see if there's anything you can do to right the wrong or make reparation. If you can't fix it—we can't fix everything—what can you learn from the mistake, and how can you make amends so that everyone involved can move on?

3. Forgive yourself. By now you know that the F-word (*forgiveness*—get your mind out of the gutter) is essential. It applies to all scenarios and circumstances, including forgiving yourself. This is an order. By this point you have cleaned up your side of the street, and no matter what, it's okay—and, in fact, it's imperative—for you to release any shame or guilt you might be carrying. Whether the other person accepts your atonement and finds peace is now up to them. I want you to take some time to

reflect on who you are inside and what was really going on with you when you did the things you regret. You're not a bad person. We all make mistakes, react angrily, screw up, and so on, and that's part of being human. Show yourself the same compassion and love you would show any other person who's in pain, and let the rest of it go. For good.

DWELL ON THE POSITIVE: THE ART OF SELF-AFFIRMATIONS

I know you're thinking right now of that old *Saturday Night Live* sketch with Al Franken, and you're giggling, right? "I'm good enough, I'm smart enough, and doggone it, people like me!" Although that sketch was absurd and hilarious, the things we think about ourselves, the things we say to ourselves in that constant inner monologue, really do affect our external lives. Remember, thoughts are *things* with dynamic power. How many times a day do you call yourself an idiot, lazy, fat, or ugly? Negative attitudes and abusive self-talk *will* sabotage your journey toward your goals. Every thought you think is a reflection of your inner truth. So this exercise is all about reprogramming: learning to replace those sniping comments with positive, loving affirmations.

And before you get giggly about the word *affirmation*, it's simply a short positive statement meant to challenge, undermine, and replace negative beliefs with a healthy, optimistic attitude that steers you toward success. What's so funny about that? It's important to construct your affirmations in just the right way. Here are the two big rules:

- Focus on only positive words and phrases. As we talked about in Chapter 2, focus on coming from a place of abundance, as you do when you are praying for something or trying to create a different outcome. Use positive words. If you use negative words, your subconscious mind will hear and place the focus on them.

• Also be sure to use the present, not the future, tense. Saying "I will be" this or "I will accomplish" that places your ideal reality in an indefinite future. Instead, tell yourself that you are this or are accomplishing that *now*. Sure, there's a little self-trickery involved, but that's the point. The goal is to get your subconscious mind to adapt and accept your affirmations *as* reality, so that they can *become* reality.

Here are some examples of what I'm talking about:

Don't say

"I will not get tired or sick during my workout today." All your brain hears is *tired, sick,* and *workout,* so that is the reality you will create: a workout that makes you tired and sick.

"I will not be afraid of making this presentation at work." Your mind picks up on the word *afraid* and focuses on it. The second you start your presentation, the fear will kick right in.

Do say

"I am strong and healthy, with the energy I need to get through my workout." This statement, using self-assured, positive language, exudes confidence that will create the outcome you desire: a strong workout that delivers results and makes you feel great.

"I am capable and prepared to give a kick-ass presentation." Your mind takes in the words *capable, prepared,* and *kick-ass,* and moves into a place of self-assurance, allowing you to relax and give a powerful presentation.

continues

Don't say

"I will make plenty of money and have the security I want and deserve." This statement puts success in an unknown, unspecified future, leaving you in a state of limbo in the present.

Do say

"I have plenty of money and the security I want and deserve." Even if you *don't* have plenty of money, if you focus on the having, rather than the lack of having, you will attach yourself to the *feeling* of having. And when your mind attaches to something so positive, look out world!

TURN IT AROUND

The idea behind this next exercise is to utilize your positive affirmations and literally create an antidote for each negative statement you hurt yourself with, thereby reversing its effects. First, make a list of all the negative things you think about and say to yourself on a regular basis. Don't hold back—get it all out on the table so we can see what we're dealing with. Now, the hard part.

Take every single one of those statements, and turn what your mind latches on to as negative into something *positive*. My favorite example for this comes from, of all places, a commercial about athletic shoes. A woman was talking about her "thunder thighs," but instead of taking it to a negative place, she turned it around by acknowledging how strong they are, how far they could carry her when she ran, and best of all, how she looked forward to bouncing her grandchildren on her powerful "thunder thighs" when she was older.

You can do this with *anything*. It can be challenging, but work at it, as often as possible. In turning things around, you are retraining your mind to support and nurture you rather than cut you down and hold you back.

Here are some other examples: Do you call yourself stupid every time you make the tiniest mistake? Back up from that strong negative language and remind yourself that *everyone* makes mistakes—it's a positive sign that you're living, doing, and being. *And* you never know where your mistakes will lead.

Work on your own list. Don't be afraid to get creative. Our minds are prone to negativity, and so it's important to be armed and ready with enough positive thinking to keep the negative hounds at bay.

HOW DO I LOVE ME? LET ME COUNT THE WAYS

It's pretty easy to rattle off a list of things we don't like about ourselves. (Don't go putting that theory to the test—just take my word for it and keep reading.) But how often have you spent any real time thinking of things about yourself that are *awesome*?

We live in a society that subtly tells us that it's better to be modest, even self-deprecating, than to acknowledge our brilliant qualities. Well, guess what: it's totally fine to feel good about yourself. This doesn't mean you think you're better than other people. It just means you appreciate and value who you are.

Living small and dumbing yourself down are not doing the world any favors. Remember, winning does not necessarily require that others lose. The fact that you think you're special doesn't mean the guy next to you isn't special, too. If you think you are great and deserving, that doesn't mean you think others are less deserving. Recognizing your strengths is healthy and an integral part of building self-esteem, so if you're feeling reluctant, GET OVER IT, and let's continue.

When I use this exercise on *The Biggest Loser,* things usually get off to a slow start because people are so afraid of appearing "boastful" or "arrogant." So I play a little game I call "I'll go first": I start with a positive statement about myself. Then it's their turn to say something they like about themselves. Once the contestants see me singing my own praises, they feel more comfortable singing theirs. So I'll go first here, too:

> I love my courage.
> I'm proud of my physique.
> I love that I'm funny. (I really am, I swear.)
> I love that I'm determined and driven.
> I love that I'm intelligent and interesting.
> I love that I'm generous and deserving of others' generosity.
> I love my eyes—they're beautiful.
> I love it that I'm a great motorcycle rider.
> I love it that I'm doing my part to change the world.
> I love my taste in nail polish.

As you can probably tell, I could go on for a while, but you probably want to finish this book at some point. So now it's your turn. Write down *at least* ten qualities you love about yourself or are proud of. Whenever you feel crappy, just go to the list and literally recite it to yourself, as a reminder that you are in fact awesome. And whenever you're feeling great, you can recite the list to remind yourself that you *really* are awesome.

I'm not going to bullshit you—this stuff isn't going to effect change overnight. It isn't magic. It will take time as well as the diligent application of everything you're learning in this book to change the way you feel about yourself and to live to your fullest potential.

But be consistent and shameless—the more often you practice these techniques, the sooner you will notice their effects. Try recording some positive affirmations and playing them while you work out. Post them on your computer desktop so you see them at work. Say them to yourself in the mirror whenever possible, especially first thing in the morning and last thing at night.

And for those of you who think this is "self-help mumbo jumbo" or are still thinking about the Al Franken skit and laughing, I ask you: how is talking shit about yourself working out for you? My guess is that it isn't. So practice saying something nice to yourself, please! Even if you don't believe in it. As I keep saying (all together now), sometimes you gotta fake it before you make it.

LEARN TO TAKE—AND GIVE— A BLOODY COMPLIMENT!

Compliments are without a doubt one of the easiest and quickest confidence-boosters out there. And yet for some reason the first thing most of us do when we receive one is to deflect it. *I like your hair.* "Oh, thanks. I couldn't do anything with it this morning." *I like your sweater.* "Oh, thanks. I'm not sure it goes with these pants." *I like your pants.* "Oh, thanks. I got them on sale."

Seriously, get over it and take the damn compliment. Even if you don't believe it, or you think it's been given out of some ulterior motive—just say thanks and accept it, own it.

On the flip side of this, *giving* compliments is another great way to project your own confidence to those around you. By giving compliments freely and genuinely, you are sending the message that you are comfortable with and enjoy other people's strengths. (Plus, it usually prompts a compliment in return, which is never a bad thing.)

REACH OUT AND HELP SOMEONE

Helping another person is one of the most powerful ways you can renew your sense of self-worth and build a healthy ego. It's a technique I use a lot on *The Biggest Loser* and *Losing It.* On season nine of *Biggest Loser,* for example, we had a contestant named Michael. If you watch the show, you may or may not remember him, but at 526 pounds, he was the heaviest contestant we'd ever had. Being the biggest contestant made him feel like the outcast of the outcasts—I saw it. But he was determined and committed to doing whatever it took to lose the weight. He listened to every word Bob and I said about nutrition, and he diligently applied the advice. He worked tirelessly in the gym and took every beating we doled out. He achieved record weight loss on campus. Basically he was a rock star. But he wasn't able to see his strengths, because the discovery of them was so new and foreign.

So one day when we were all in the gym, I noticed another contestant, Ashley, struggling to run her sprints. I asked Michael to help motivate her through it. He was shocked. I was asking *him* to *help* someone? He was the heaviest person there—what did he possibly have to offer anyone? At first he protested, but I insisted. So Michael set out to "coach Ashley," while I continued training my other contestants. He was successful in helping her, and when the day was over, he was walking on air.

By empowering Michael to help someone else, I indirectly conveyed to him that he was knowledgeable, that he had talents and abilities that were valuable. Helping Ashley gave him a greater sense of purpose and significance, and for the first time he was able to see his true power. He realized that Ashley's success was in part inspired by *his* strength, knowledge, and motivation. He left the gym that day a changed man, feeling the true breadth of his potential. And do I even need to tell you, or did you already guess (or watch it)? Michael went on to win the show and lose the most weight in *Biggest Loser* history.

When you help someone, you are implicitly acknowledging, and allowing it to be acknowledged, that you are *good* at something, that you have knowledge and experience to impart, and that you can in your own small way help make the world a better place.

Now, for those of you struggling with pretty low self-esteem, I have to be very clear about one thing: helping people is not to be confused with codependency, or helping others to your own detriment. This is about paying it forward and being comfortable in knowing that you've got enough to give some back. Many of our contestants go on from the show to become trainers themselves, whether formally or informally. They go back home healthy and strong and can't help but educate their family, friends, and in many cases their entire community about healthy living.

Koli from season nine was a great football player, so he decided to coach little kids. Pete from season two became a fitness trainer. Michelle from season six went on to become an inspirational speaker empowering women around the country. I could go on and on. The fact is that doing this kind of work keeps people on the straight and narrow and reminds them daily of their competence and value.

I want *you* to think about the things that you are good at and the simple ways you can help people in the day-to-day. When it comes to building self-worth, very few things are as empowering and intoxicating. And I guarantee that helping others will ultimately be one of the most powerful actions you can take in helping yourself.

ESTEEM BOOSTERS: TIPS, TRICKS, AND TREATS

- **Get something personal done that you have been putting off.** The simplest act of taking care of yourself can go a long way in the self-esteem department. Even if it's something as mundane as doing laundry, cleaning out your closet, or cooking yourself a wholesome dinner instead of ordering takeout, you are sending a message to yourself that you are worth spending time on and capable of being good to yourself.
- **Exercise!** Of course for me this is huge—I've written whole books on the subject. Exercise *dramatically enhances* your confidence in a number of ways. It makes you feel better about how you look; it releases mood-boosting chemicals in the brain, making you feel better about life in general; and it makes a statement, to yourself and the world, that you are

worth taking good care of. Ultimately, when you feel strong physically, you feel strong in other aspects of your life as well.

- **Keep up with doctor and dentist appointments, and remember that hygiene is keen.** Simple things like keeping your nails trimmed, your teeth white, and your hair cut and healthy make you feel more attractive. Taking care of your health by getting your yearly checkup or biannual teeth cleaning will make you feel significant and reinforce that you matter. When you don't look after yourself in these ways, it's neglect. Neglect, either by yourself or by someone else (the one will usually lead to the other), makes you feel inadequate. Don't stand for it. You are important—treat yourself accordingly.

- **Speak up!** This may sound crazy, but if there's one thing I've seen work again and again, it's taking a course in public speaking. You may dread getting up in front of people, but there's no better way to jump-start your belief in your own abilities than to become comfortable communicating ideas to people. By taking a course, you will be assured a safe environment where everyone is learning. Even if you never have to speak in public, the things you learn can apply to communication in all aspects of your life.

- **Celebrate your friends.** Have an appreciation session with your friends or loved ones. Take some time to talk about the things you value about each other. It may sound a little cheesy, but it really works, and everyone ends up feeling good.

- **Smile!** This is one of the simplest and most powerful acts of kindness. There's actually a special theory that backs me up—the facial feedback theory. Facial expressions send very strong messages to our brains—no big surprise. So when people smile at us, friends, strangers, coworkers, whoever, it's a small but significant boost to our sense of worth. If you smile at someone, they are most likely going to smile back. Making a conscious effort to smile more on a day-to-day basis will make you more content and confident in the long run.

You've just gotten through the most intense section of the book, the one that requires the most from your heart and your head. Step One was the magical part, where you got to free yourself and spend some time in your imagination. Step Two was hard! It's where most of your real work began and will continue long after you put the book down. (Just so you know, Step Three is as simple as following instructions, but we're not finished here yet.)

I told you from the word go that this work would require some serious courage on your part. But nothing ventured, nothing gained. If you don't do this work, you will suffocate under the weight of your self-loathing and baggage; you must face down these demons or your life will remain unfulfilled.

Don't be the blind man clinging to the wall. Have you ever heard that saying "Fearing death is fearing life"? Constantly avoiding, denying, negating, or neglecting due to fear is a spiritual death. For that reason, this is the most worthwhile work you will ever do.

So now that this work is under way, it's time for you to take some risks, get uncomfortable, and really embrace life. Let me remind you: when I talk about taking risks, I'm not asking you to volunteer for acts of stupidity or bravado. I'm talking about taking smart, calculated risks. I'm talking about making sure you are as set up for success as is humanly possible. Again, this is not to say you won't fail—believe me, you will. Lord knows I have. We all do. But the agenda here is positive results and change for the better.

Think of it this way: let's say you're afraid of heights. You decide you want to conquer this fear by going skydiving. Do you muster up the courage one day, haul off, and jump out of a plane at max altitude? HELL, NO. Or at least I sincerely hope not. First, you do research on the sport, identifying the best company to go with, the best equipment to use, the safest places to do it. You find an instructor you trust who teaches you how to pack your chute. You have a backup chute just in case. You survey the topography to make sure you're not jumping into a forest, mountains, or the ocean. Only when you have analyzed the situation, minimized the risk factors, and taken all steps to ensure success, then and only then do you jump.

It may sound like common sense, but when it comes to our lives, we often just show up, jump, and pay the price later for our lack of preparedness. Well, no more. You need to apply the same kind of focus and planning to the leap you're making here. And this is what the next section is all about: bringing deliberate thought and strategic action to all your best intentions, to ensure the greatest possibility of success. Let's get ready to jump.

STEP THREE

ACHIEVE

At this point you should take a moment to acknowledge the fact that you've come a long way. You've learned how to figure out what it is you want. And you've learned how to do the internal work to go after it full force.

Awesome!

Now what?

As I'm sure you know, no one has succeeded just by thinking positively and feeling good about themselves. To succeed in life, you have to take action. But how? What's the first step? Taking action without focus is a recipe for disaster. Luckily, you don't have to worry about that. Step Three is all about the specific moves you can make in order to go after your dream. Some of the things I talk about will apply more to the professional side of life, some more to the personal, but whatever part of your life you are focusing on, I'm going to give you the tools you need to achieve everything you have in mind and more.

But first, let's go back to school . . .

CHAPTER NINE

HIT THE BOOKS—THEN THE DECK

We will change anything if we feel that it's worth it and that we are able. Ability is where the education aspect of this plan comes into play. Ninety-nine point nine percent of the time we fail because we were improperly prepared. You're not lazy, you weren't born under a bad sign, and your genetics have not sentenced you to a life of failure. You may simply have been unable to move forward because you didn't yet *know how;* you didn't have enough information on what to do.

The solution lies in continued learning. Whether it's learning from your mistakes or learning something totally new, every bit of knowledge you gain is an extra tool for growth and for meeting new problems and working them out.

Knowledge truly is power. With the right information, you can make informed choices that will help steer any outcome in your favor. Education brings focus to all your endeavors, and in professional settings it gives you the edge over your competition. Without it, your actions can become like a wrecking ball, out of control and potentially counterproductive. So be sure to learn everything there is to know about the goal you are hoping to achieve. Don't wait for it to come your way—pursue it. Here are a few ways to start.

DO YOUR HOMEWORK

Before you pursue any endeavor, do your homework! Much as in our skydiving analogy in Chapter 8, getting informed allows you to plan an advantageous course of action that helps keep you out of harm's way *and* helps ensure results. Planning isn't hard or costly. All it requires is a little diligence and patience. Spend time studying up on the subject you are about to pursue. Read books on the topic, watch documentaries, listen to podcasts, and search the Internet. Technology provides countless resources for information on almost anything. You may not have direct access to an expert, but the great thing about today's technology is, you're not reliant on others to get you the info you need.

You can't imagine how many people come up to me on a daily basis, discouraged and overwhelmed, and tell me they "can't lose weight." They are misinformed. Every human being can lose weight—it's part of our genetic makeup. The key is addressing how they're going about it. When I ask them questions, it becomes clear to me that they aren't educated about the scientific facts of weight loss and so aren't able to take effective action.

They don't know how many calories to eat, how many calories they are burning, how various foods affect their natural metabolism, and so on. After I teach them Weight Loss 101, they are able to make the proper food and exercise choices so that the weight falls off. This information is out there, however, and they could have saved themselves years of struggle and heartache had they bothered to look for it.

I can hear some of you right now: *I've bought book after book, followed fad diet after fad diet, and still not gotten results or "right" information?!* If you're thinking that, you bring up a great point. There's so much conflicting info out there, how do you know which sources to trust?

Seek out information from reliable sources that have a proven track record. And always look for evidence, facts, and testimonials that back up and validate the credibility of that information.

For example, if I want to learn about snowboarding, I'm first going to see if Shaun White has a book, video game, DVD, or podcast on the topic. Considering that he is an Olympic gold medalist in the sport, I feel that qualifies him as one of the foremost experts. Same with Roger Federer and tennis, Meryl Streep and acting, Suze Orman and money. In other words, don't take diet advice from your brother-in-law, for God's sake! Unless of course he's a registered dietitian or a certified fitness trainer. By seeking out knowledge from the foremost authority on the topic, someone who delivers tangible results consistently, you buy yourself huge peace of mind.

Sometimes you might find more than one authority offering "more than one way to skin a cat." That's another reason that being well versed in a subject is critical. You want to ingest all the information you can, apply it to your unique personality, and then pick the course of action that is right for you.

In most cases, the path to knowledge is fairly well established and straightforward, whether it's medicine, law, or snowboarding; but in certain instances, as with weight loss, you will come across shysters. And where you find half-truths and misinformation, you will always find greed. If something sounds too good to be true, IT IS! Use your common sense, and trust your gut to weed out bullshit. We *all* know that you can't eat anything you want and lose weight, there's no miracle pill that replaces exercise, and you can't just take the stairs. Don't look for shortcuts. Be prepared to put in the time and work. Ninety-nine percent of the time we allow ourselves to be misled because someone has played upon our apathy, but they can sell you a crock only if you're willing to buy it.

Having the *proper* knowledge before taking action is a critical factor in whether you succeed or fail. It doesn't matter how you get the information—from a person, book, Internet, DVD, radio, or podcast. The answers *are* out there. Seek them out, and then use them as tools to improve the effectiveness of your choices and the quality of your life.

TAKE A HISTORY LESSON

Sometimes we can overlook the importance of knowing the history of whatever business, craft, or endeavor we want to master. Are there experts that you can study? Are there statistics and trends you can track? Have there been changes over time that you should be aware of? Every generation builds upon the knowledge of the last, and the more you know about what's transpired in the past, the more equipped you are to kick butt in the present and be an innovator in the future.

For a very clear example, let's look at the world of astronomy. (I'm not sure you want to go out and become a physicist or cosmologist, but bear with me, you'll see where I'm going.) For hundreds of years people believed the earth was the center of everything. Then Copernicus came along in the sixteenth century and posited the heliocentric model of the universe, in which we revolved around the sun, not the other way around. After that, somewhere around 1610, Galileo came along, built the first telescope—minor accomplishment—and corroborated Copernicus's theory. But he made one small change: the sun was the center of our solar system, he said, but not our universe. Then Kepler came up with the laws of planetary motion, which he based on the observations made by astronomers who'd come before him. A century later Sir Isaac Newton built on that to arrive at his theory of gravitation. Then Einstein shook that theory up with his work on relativity. *Then* Stephen Hawking came on the scene with his groundbreaking studies of the big bang and black holes. Today theoretical physicists are pondering a "theory of everything," or an ultimate explanation of nature, or reality, studying new and exciting fields like string theory and membrane theory.

I'm not trying to give you a headache with all this physics talk; I'm trying to illustrate how a field evolves over time, and each new development is made possible by the study of what came before. Yes, starting your own clothing business (to take just one example) isn't exactly discovering the keys to the universe. But the same principles apply. If I hadn't studied what came before me in the field of nutrition and dietary science, I never could have written *Master Your Metabolism*. (But having a world-class endocrinologist and medical researcher as writing partners didn't hurt either!) So take note: if you want to rise to the top of your field, study it so that you can expand, revise, and innovate!

SOMEONE TO WATCH OVER ME

Having a mentor can save you a lot of time and accelerate your success. In most things we undertake, there's no guidebook telling us what to study, what to master, and in what order. If we are new to something, figuring out what skills to hone and what action to take can be a difficult task. As you start out, there's nothing wrong with asking for help and guidance from those wiser than you. I guarantee you that a lot of the most powerful, successful people you can think of did so, too.

I'll tell you a personal story. My business partner, Giancarlo Chersich (affectionately known as G.C.), and I met and connected with Suze Orman through a speaking engagement she and I were signed up for in 2008. Although the event ended up never happening, G.C. and I were fortunate enough to have Suze and her partner, K.T., take us under their wings. Suze counseled us on all kinds of amazingly useful things, from working with QVC to protecting ourselves legally. She warned us that as I got more high profile, litigious people would "inevitably" look to make a quick buck by filing lawsuits against our company. She advised us to get something called an "errors and omissions" insurance policy to cover legal costs in the event of such a lawsuit, and to make sure we were indemnified with all our partners (meaning they would cover our legal costs).

Sure enough, eighteen months later we found ourselves in a baseless lawsuit, and her advice turned out to be incredibly useful and prophetic. Suze counsels us to this day, thank God, and even advised me on the best time of year to release this book you are currently reading. Finding a good mentor is not easy, so let's go over a few strategies to help you find your match.

What do you need? What kind of guidance do you want? Do you need advice, introductions, and networking help? Or do you want someone who can listen and be neutral and helpful when times are trying? If you narrow your focus, it will be easier to find someone who can help you in the way you need it most.

Make a list. With the above in mind, identify experts that have the qualities you are looking for. It's important here to keep an open mind and consider a wide range of people. Someone you may not have originally thought of could turn out to be exactly the mentor you need. He or she may be able to help you in ways you hadn't expected, or in ways you didn't think you needed. Mentors come in many forms. Your immediate circle of friends and family is the place to start your search, and from there you can move on to teachers and coworkers. If you belong to any groups, what about looking to the group's leader? Do you have a spiritual guide in your life? Really think about everyone among your acquaintances, since it's always easier to approach someone you know than someone you don't, although don't rule out the idea of contacting strangers out of the blue. This brings me to my next point.

Decide on your approach. Have a game plan in place and a script ready before you ask a person to mentor you. If you don't already know them, start by learning a little about them so you get an idea of how you can put your best foot forward and be taken the most seriously. Think about how you are going to contact them: by phone, e-mail, written letter, a lunch, a meeting, and so on. Explain why you've chosen the person, and what type of advice you're looking for. If the person is not able to help you, don't be discouraged. Ask for suggestions of other people who might, or just thank the person for their time and move on. Above all stay positive and open. The right person will come when the time is right.

Aspire to be the person you admire. The people you most look up to may be inaccessible to you for one reason or another. I realized pretty early on in my career that Oprah was probably too busy to take a reality-show fitness trainer under her wing. So maybe I couldn't have coffee with her—but I *could* study her and learn *from* her by learning *about* her. Studying the life stories and trajectories of people who have achieved things you want is a very powerful educational tool, not to be underestimated. Aspiration is elusive without role models. Master chess players are famous for studying historical matches between old masters until they are cross-eyed, comparing moves they might have made and identifying mistakes.

Don't limit yourself to just one role model. Times change, and individual circumstances or random acts of serendipity must be taken into account. I've studied the careers of fitness gurus, self-help masters, brand builders, journalists, and pop culture messengers—everyone from Jane Fonda and Richard Simmons to Martha Stewart, Oprah Winfrey, Anthony Robbins, Eleanor Roosevelt, and Barbara Walters. The list goes on. All of these people have achieved goals that I aspire to, and reading up on them has guided and inspired me again and again. How did they get their start? How did they build their success? What was their trajectory? That helped me know what steps to put first in my process and which to leave out entirely.

This technique, by the way, applies to anything you choose to pursue, whether it's in your career or your personal life. Let's say your goal is to lose weight. Look to people you know who have been successful. Maybe you know a colleague who has recently lost fifty pounds. Ask questions about their process, what worked for them, how they got through the plateaus, how often they exercised, what kinds of exercises were most effective, what foods they avoided, and so on.

SPREAD YOUR BETS

As you gain knowledge in your area, remember that your objective is not just to amass information, but to wrangle it all into some sort of system that will help you move toward your goal. When you study those who have been successful, pay particular attention to the order of events as they happened. Martha Stewart worked at *Family Circle* magazine, one of the most successful magazines in its category, for five years before starting her own magazine, *Martha Stewart Living*. No doubt her five years there taught her much that helped her make *Martha Stewart Living* a huge success. I've chosen to follow that model in my own career as well. A couple of years ago I was given the opportunity to start my own magazine, but with Martha Stewart's trajectory in mind, I decided to pass. Instead, I accepted an offer to be a contributing editor to *Self*, the most successful women's health magazine on the market today. I realized that it would probably be better in the long run to align myself with a top "book" in my field, learn from the best, and *then* strike out on my own when the time was right.

Now, an important caveat. For many reasons, don't limit yourself to following a single model. You have to be able to stay current and forward thinking as the world changes. This is a fluid universe, and you must always be ready to revise your knowledge and adapt your game plan. In my magazine example, I'm realizing now that in today's environmental, economic, and technological climate, more and more of us are seeking information and entertainment online, and the paper magazine is becoming a dinosaur. Declining ad revenue is forcing many magazines to fold. So a Jillian Michaels magazine may not be in my future after all. Times have changed since Martha's success, and I'm respecting that, adapting accordingly, and currently choosing instead to focus on my website content at JillianMichaels.com.

Learning everything you can about your field is absolutely key as a first step to achieving what you want. When you are informed, you have the ability to act powerfully, in a way that effects true, lasting change. Without knowledge, you will fail over and over because your actions will lack merit. So your next step is pretty simple: you gotta practice. Practicing means applying what you learn. If you want to lose weight, you have to practice weight-loss behaviors. You have to practice healthy cooking and working out in order to enhance your effectiveness at those things. If you want to be at the top of your professional field, you have to practice the relevant skills. Practice does make perfect, but only if you are practicing the right things in the right way.

PRACTICE, PRACTICE, PRACTICE

I bet you're thinking, *Practice. That's obvious. I'll skim this part.* Think again. This section is a long one, for good reason. There are many pivotal components to this concept, so buck up and pay attention. The traditional assumption is that we are born with certain talents or a lack thereof, and that brands us for life. This is simply not true. No characteristic of the brain or body constrains us from reaching almost any level of achievement. This is why practice is so important.

Say you want to go back to school—you should practice test taking and writing skills. Say you want to become more assertive at your current job; you need to practice communication and cooperation skills. It seems obvious, but there's a catch: putting in hours of plain old hard work like your grandmother told you to isn't going to cut it. It might make you okay, maybe even good, but it won't make you great.

Greatness requires a much more specific kind of work—what we'll call *target practice*.

Target practice means taking action to work SMARTER as well as harder in pursuit of your goals. I also refer to this work as *specific practice*. But before we get into all that, let's establish exactly what you're going to focus your energy on. What is it that you are practicing?

Are you wondering what the hell I'm talking about? Maybe you're thinking, *Easy. I want to practice tennis so I can improve my game.* Okay, that's true, but what aspects of your game are you going to put your energy into? More specifically, what aspects of the game do you have the *power* to improve? It's no good worrying about who your opponent is going to be, or whether they will be better, stronger, or faster than you. But you can focus on your serve, your backhand, and your net play, thus being proactive and making yourself stronger for any opponent who might come along.

So when looking at what to practice, you have to focus your efforts on things you have the power to change and improve. Often we think that the outside world has to change before we can. *If only I had a better boss . . . If only I had my degree . . . If only there were more job opportunities, then I'd have a better career. If only I were thin, then I would fall in love. If only there were a gym closer to my house, I'd work out more. If only, if only, if only . . .*

This reactive mode of thinking will get you nowhere fast. Reactive people focus on other people and on external circumstances over which they have no control. This is fruitless and serves only to drain your valuable energy and contribute to feelings of hopelessness, inadequacy, and victimization. Without a proactive focus, you will find yourself in that dreaded loop where you continue to make the same mistakes over and over again. If something truly is out of your control, no matter how hard or how smart you work, the likelihood is that it will remain unchangeable by you.

QUIZ
Are You
Proactive or
Reactive?

The real path to success lies in knowing how to change yourself from the inside out. What can you work on *right now* to make your situation better? Can you be more patient, determined, creative, positive, knowledgeable, or flexible? By using a proactive focus, you direct your energies toward practicing the things you can change, which will help you gain control of most situations and, ultimately, your life.

For example, suppose you want to lose weight, but your family is always eating junk food around you. What should you do? You can try talking to your family and getting them to change their eating habits. But what if they don't? Even if they do, how will you control your coworkers who are eating crap around you, or the strangers at restaurants who sit next to you? You really can't. The solution is to focus on you. Create different active-family quality times that aren't about food, like challenging each other to Wii tennis every night instead of watching TV. At work, try bringing in healthy snacks for your coworkers, and instead of happy hour start a walking group and see who joins. If people don't get on your bandwagon, set healthy boundaries and continue to perfect the things you can control, as that will set you up for success.

It's not what happens to you, but your response to what happens to you, that makes or breaks you in this life. By changing your responses, you change the end result. Don't spend your life reacting to the emotional lives and behavior of others, thereby allowing their weaknesses to control you. Instead focus on your own actions and values. *That* is where true freedom and accomplishment lie.

MASTER OF YOUR UNIVERSE

High achievement is not reserved for a chosen few. Despite prevailing beliefs that certain people are born gifted while others are doomed to languish in mediocrity, current research is showing us that this *isn't* the case. In studying modern-day "prodigies," psychologists and others have found few signs of extraordinary achievement before the subjects began intensive training. This means, in short, that anyone can master anything they choose if they work hard enough for it. Yes, the price is high, but greatness is within all of us.

I know what you're thinking, because I thought it, too: *Bullshit. Some people are born with physical or mental attributes that allow them to excel at certain things.* While this is true in some specific cases—yes, if you're five foot two, you probably won't be playing pro ball for a living—in most, it's not.

We are all born with attributes that we can develop, be they physical or mental. Most of the time, the way we live and work alters our nature and development. For instance, for a long time many people thought Lance Armstrong was a great biker, in part because of his oversize heart. But now they are saying that it's the other way around, that endurance training will cause the heart of an athlete to grow (in this case a good thing), in adaptation to the strenuous demands put upon it. After they stop training, their hearts return to average size.

Baseball players develop the ability to extend their throwing arms farther back than regular Joes, through years of practice. Athletes have the ability to change not only the size of their muscles but their composition as well, depending on the sport they are practicing. We can develop more of the fast-twitch, explosive-strength fibers for sports like sprinting and Olympic lifting, or we can develop more slow-twitch endurance-muscle fiber for sports like marathon running.

This goes for our brains as well. The areas of our brains that are repeatedly stimulated produce more of a special coating, called myelin, that facilitates the smooth, rapid transmission of electrochemical messages between the components of the central nervous system and the rest of the body. So things we repeat can become "second nature."

Even the territories of our brains can be reassigned. The brains of children who diligently practice music literally develop differently. The regions of their brains that control tones and control fingers take over more territory. Fascinating stuff, right?

TARGET PRACTICE

The fact that we can physically and mentally adapt in these ways means that almost nothing is beyond the scope of our capabilities—the key is harder, smarter work. Target practice.

Target practice, however, is not just about the adaptations that help us achieve success. It's also about developing skills, methods, and strategies to use in conjunction with any attributes you may augment.

The key components of target practice are goal deconstruction, constant self-examination and monitoring, and immediate feedback from yourself and others. You are still going to put in the hours of hard work, but you will zero in on your weaknesses so you can overcome them and blast through all obstacles.

The sad truth is that most people practice the same things over and over, and while they may become good, they never become great. In fact, some studies have shown that an entire lifetime working at something doesn't necessarily make us better and in some cases can actually make us worse. I know doctors, lawyers, trainers—you name it—who have been working in their profession for years but aren't at the top of their field. They might be putting in the hours, but often they are just spending a lot of time making the same mistakes over and over, getting discouraged, and becoming apathetic.

That's why the *how* of practice is so important. It can mean the difference between achievement and stagnation. It doesn't matter what you're practicing: your jump shot, finding your soul mate, or anything in between. You probably don't think that practicing applies to getting a healthy emotional connection with a loved one or controlling impulsivity—but you *should*. Doing specific practice in these areas means taking effective action, analyzing the results or your progress, and learning from your mistakes. It will add up to greatness no matter what aspect of your life you're practicing.

The process can be tiring, and it leaves *no* room for ego, but it works. If you want to take your life to new heights, you must learn how to apply this technique to your endeavors. Let's take a look at the first step: breaking it down.

BREAK IT DOWN

We've all heard this advice a million times: "Take it one step at a time." There's a reason why we keep hearing it: it's spot-on accurate.

The best performers realize that the key to success is breaking down an overall goal into components and focusing on perfecting the components rather than the end result. Focus on the process, not the goal. To take an easy example, musicians will practice a fragment of a piece again and again until they have mastered it, then move on to the next fragment, and the next, and so on. Only after they've mastered all the sections do they string them together and play the whole piece. Fluency happens after each component is mastered individually. Only then are we able to process them all simultaneously and perform them with excellence. *That's* what gives rise to greatness.

Now let's take a less conventional example, like working on a relationship. Your overall goal is for the relationship to be happy and healthy. But there are a lot of components to a happy, healthy relationship: you need to know how to listen, how to communicate, how to compromise, how to forgive, and so on. Let's say you're a good listener but a lousy communicator—this is where you start practicing.

Evaluate the weakness. Do you keep everything bottled up and expect telepathy when it comes to others understanding your needs? Do you get defensive and start yelling when you should remain calm and talk things through? Do you put others on the defensive without meaning to by expressing yourself in "you" statements rather than "I" statements? (As in "You are an inconsiderate jerk for not calling to tell me you would be late," rather than "When you don't let me know you are running late, it makes me feel worried about your safety and insignificant to you as well.")

Breaking down your goal lets you focus your energy on the weaker areas that are holding you back. Once you have mastered one weak spot, you're ready to move on to the next. Tiger Woods smartly uses target practice to enhance his golf game. He doesn't just play one round of golf after another. He picks a shot he's struggling with—say, hitting the ball out of a sand trap from an incredibly difficult line—and works on that specific shot until it improves. This strategy of breaking down the things we need to practice into individual components makes the overall goal of improvement less daunting and more digestible and helps us make the best use of our time. By just doing one small thing at a time, we systematically eliminate the obstacles that hold us back, rather than getting overwhelmed by everything we need to get better at.

Okay, so now you're thinking, *Great, Jillian. Break down our weaknesses and work on the stuff we suck at, but how?* Read on—the answer lies in using immediate feedback and repetition.

GET LOOPED IN

I covered this subject earlier in this chapter when I talked about the benefits of having a mentor. But I'm hitting it again because a key principle of practice is that we must learn from what we do, and the quickest way to do that is to seek out immediate feedback from someone with proven expertise. That way you know right away when you are off course, you learn from your mistakes, and you bring improved strategy to your methods.

You may be thinking, *I don't need outside feedback. I know when I'm on the right track and when I'm not.* If I had a dollar for every person whose life was a mess who said to me, "I don't need therapy, I know what my problems are," I'd be kickin' it with my neighbor Bill Gates.

But the truth is, often we are too close to a situation to see it for what it really is. How many times have you thought you nailed a job interview only to find out someone else got the gig? Or been dumped by a boyfriend when you thought things were going really well? Sometimes it really helps to get the advice of a friend, coach, or mentor to help us figure out where we are falling short and how we can fix it.

Let's take a few hypothetical examples. If Tiger Woods is struggling to hit a ball out of a sand trap, a coach might recognize that he is using the wrong golf club for the shot or possibly that he needs to angle his body differently. If you're not advancing at work, a colleague or supervisor might be able to tell you about a mistake you're making that's holding you back. A loved one might point out something that is straining your relationship. This type of feedback saves us hours of frustration and the pain of failure.

Think about it—people don't try to learn sports on their own. Most CEOs, when they are facing a challenge, call in advisers. Doctors spend years interning under seasoned professionals. And so on. Seeking real-time feedback from an expert can save you much time and struggle and increases your chances of success exponentially. I have been able to help so many people break through years of diet mistakes in just a few short minutes, simply by analyzing what they've been doing, pointing out the mistakes, and giving them the proper information to apply so they can lose weight.

Again, whom you seek advice from will depend on what area you're looking to improve in, but common sense will usually dictate whom to get feedback from. Sometimes it's obvious. If you want to learn how to get in shape, get a trainer. If you're looking to climb the ladder at work with an eye to getting a better job and salary, then ask your boss what you could be doing better. If you want to improve your relationship with a loved one, ask what you could be doing differently, or discuss the problem with a therapist or a trusted friend.

In almost everything you could want to do, there's a way to get feedback from somebody who knows more than you do—all you have to do is toughen up and have the courage to listen. No one really likes to hear criticism, even if it's constructive. But at the end of the day, you're talking about a momentary sting versus the anguish and confusion of repeating the same mistakes again and again. Man up. Be *grateful* for the knowledge. Take it to heart and soar.

Now, you don't have to, nor should you, rely on other people as your sole source of feedback. Self-assessment is going to play a big part in your progress as well. This brings us to our next step, which even has a fancy name: metacognition.

LET ME THINK ON IT: UNDERSTANDING METACOGNITION

Metacognition is one of the current buzzwords in the field of educational psychology and is often defined as thinking about thinking. I know right now you are thinking, *Huh?* But all it means for our purposes is being brave enough to step outside yourself and evaluate your behaviors and actions honestly, so that you can make improvements. In Step Two, I hammered into you that you must learn from your failures in order to improve. Metacognition is paramount in helping you do that.

Metacognitive skills include planning and selecting strategies, analyzing their effectiveness, correcting errors, and changing methods when necessary. Those with greater metacognitive skills are more successful in their endeavors. Period. The good news is that we can all cultivate these skills, and here I'll tell you how.

There are two parts to it. The first is taking responsibility. I've touched on responsibility in other parts of the book, but it applies here, too. One of the traits of highly successful people is their belief that they take responsibility for their mistakes. They don't blame their setbacks on the other guy getting lucky, or on genetic inferiority, or on a freak of circumstance; instead they shine a light on those setbacks to see what they can learn from them and how they can adapt their performance to avoid similar setbacks in the future. Now, for this you have to learn to become aware of your actions in a way you probably haven't been up until now.

As you practice, you must be conscious and honest with yourself about where you are struggling and what you need to do better. You can monitor yourself by asking a few simple questions after every practice:

What did I do well?

What could I have done better?

Was there a turning point in my performance for better or worse? And if so, what were the direct causes or surrounding circumstances?

How did my thoughts, emotions, and reactions contribute to my success or failure?

Look at your answers impersonally and judiciously. Take out your journal, or go online to my website, but write the facts down. Make note of the problems, as well as the ambiguities and inconsistencies, that are holding you back. Then jot down how you can start to deal with them. Once you start thinking impartially about your work, you'll be amazed how your mind will jump to the challenge of figuring out where and how to improve a weakness. This type of self-monitoring allows you to zero in on the areas that need strengthening when you don't have a coach or a mentor.

The second key to metacognition is to stay present and maintain concentration. Since life doesn't always play out the way we expect it to, it's important to be aware and to monitor our thoughts and actions so we can easily adapt to changing circumstances. If something that is out of your control goes wrong, how are you going to change your game plan to avoid being torpedoed? In adverse circumstances, the last thing you want to do is act on impulse or emotion or, even worse, not react at all. By slowing down, taking in the situation, and thinking through the choices you are about to make, you help ensure that the outcome will be in your favor.

On *The Biggest Loser*, you can see this at work. The most successful contestants are those who are always thinking, processing, and applying the information that Bob and I give them. While others are unraveling, zoning out, or complaining about the pain, these contestants stay present and think about their breathing, focus on their form, visualize their goals, and remind themselves why they are there and what their greater purpose is. It's this kind of thinking that separates the good from the great.

As you become more skilled at using metacognitive strategies, you will gain confidence and become more independent as a learner, and more successful in your practice.

As if taking criticism from others and giving it to ourselves weren't hard enough, once you have figured out the areas where you need work and the activities you need to do, you must do them over and over again. Remember, I never said this would be easy. Possible, yes; easy, no. This is probably why so few people achieve greatness. It's tough! When I meet couples who have been together for years and years, one of the first questions I always ask is, "How do you guys do it?" Without fail, every single one of them has the same answer: "It's hard! We work at it!"

Success is always within your reach. How badly do you want it? If your answer is "A LOT," then get ready for the next step, which is about repetition, repetition, repetition.

REPEAT AFTER ME

Repetition is the fourth critical part of target practice. You can know what changes you need to make and where your weaknesses lie, but unless you practice over and over, you're simply not going to see more than incremental improvement. It takes a lot of time and enormous effort to become a master. Some theorists have even posited the "ten-year rule," which states (as its name implies) that it takes a decade of work in anything before one can truly be a master. Even child prodigies, such as Carl Friedrich Gauss in mathematics, Mozart in music, and Bobby Fischer in chess, must have made an equivalent effort, perhaps by starting earlier and working harder and smarter than others. Studies show that world-class experts, whether chess prodigies or musical virtuosi, practice at least three to five hours a day. WOW.*

A big part of practicing successfully has to do with that substance that's produced in the brain, myelin. Every time you practice something, you are literally carving neurological pathways in your brain, and as you repeat it, it becomes more automatic.

This process can work for you when you are practicing things the right way, but it can work against you if you are practicing them the wrong way. That's why target practice is so important. It allows you to work on perfecting mistakes as opposed to ingraining them. In addition, target practice requires that you constantly push yourself just out of your comfort zone (i.e., working on the stuff you suck at) to continue improving your abilities. In other words, once you have mastered something, it's time to get out of your comfort zone and practice a new aspect of your skill that has been challenging you.

Think of it like this. If a child's goal is mobility, first he would master crawling, then walking, jogging, running, and sprinting, and eventually even hill sprints. No one is meant to repeat crawling over and over again. We all need to continue practicing and repeating, but only when we are in our "learning zone"—working on things that are just outside our reach.

Now, a final word: be patient with yourself, and don't be afraid. You don't have to lose yourself in pursuit of your goal—whether it's to find a life partner, make some money doing something you love, or anything else you might want. I'm just pointing out the importance of putting in the amount and type of work that comes with achieving something you want. Sure, it's daunting, but it's also empowering. It literally changes you from the inside out. Let's look a little deeper at these physiological effects by briefly exploring the concept of cognitive mapping.

* Philip E. Ross, "The Expert Mind," *Scientific American* (July 24, 2006).

MAP IT OUT

Research has shown that behavior is deeply ingrained in actual physical pathways in the brain. All of your beliefs and habits, everything making up your mental reality, is contained in these neural connections. Each time you take an action or think a thought, it is communicated to your neurons via tiny electrochemical messages.

The first time you have an experience or learn something new, a new pathway is created. Then the next time you have that experience, your brain will search to see if you have experienced it before. If you have, the experience will follow the same pathway. This is where the myelination effect I discussed earlier comes into play. The more often you engage in a behavior or think a thought, the stronger the neural pathway holding that thought or behavior will become. This is how a thought or action becomes habit—a habit is more a cemented highway than a pathway. That's why the repetition aspect of specific practice is so important. It helps create strong highways that your brain can map to make the skill set associated with your goal habitual and automatic.

Immediate feedback is important because it keeps you from reinforcing negative patterns, actions, or behaviors that get you stuck in a rut, literally. So the final nail in the structure of specific practice is to undo your bad habits by altering these neural pathways. You can override the old bad habit by wiring a new behavior or thought pattern—another reason that continued learning is so critical to your success. When you create new, constructive pathways, the old, destructive ones atrophy. As in, they go away! By refusing to indulge in negative thoughts or self-destructive behaviors, over time you weaken their hold over you.

We can't talk about cognitive mapping without bringing our emotions into the discussion. We are sensitive, feeling beings, and our emotions carry a lot of weight. If we are going to remap our inner landscape and replace destructive habits with effective, successful ones, we need to manipulate our emotions so that they are working for us, not against us.

If something feels good, you're likely to do it again. If something doesn't feel good, chances aren't super that you're going to go back for more. So how do we get ourselves to repeatedly engage in behaviors that may not be instantly gratifying? By focusing on your emotional attachment to the end result.

Let's use a simple example. Let's say you hate running. I do. I *hate* it. I also don't exactly love steamed veggies. That said, I'm on the treadmill running most days of the week, and I'm eating up my beans and greens just as often. Why? Because I *love* that the running and the broccoli help me fit into my skinny jeans, which makes me feel sexy. I love that they give me more confidence. I love that after engaging in these healthy behaviors, I feel energized and in a good mood.

By focusing on these hugely positive results and my attachment to them, I'm able to change the associations my brain makes with these objects. Instead of associating running on the treadmill with boredom, fatigue, and agony, I'm associating it with strength, health, and sexiness! By forming these new, positive associations with certain behaviors, we create strong cognitive maps that ingrain these behaviors into habit.

And by forming a positive emotional association with certain objects around you, you're more inclined to be successful. Objects in our environment can strongly influence what we think and practice, as we'll see in Chapter 10. But gearing your environment for success is crucial, and manipulating yourself to see healthy objects that might normally make you cringe in a beneficial light is a perfect example.

In the above instance, we have:

Treadmill = looking awesome in skinny jeans, more energy,
     better sex life
Broccoli = disease prevention, years of quality living

Such associations also work in reverse. I want you to start attributing hurtful things like junk food, alcohol, cigarettes, and maybe even credit cards (if spending is your problem) with the negative, dark emotions they cause in the long term, even if they provide momentary pleasure:

Burger and fries = muffin top, lethargy, self-loathing, muu-muus
Credit card and late-night Internet shopping = fear, debt, anxiety
Alcohol = lack of productivity, hangover, regret
Cigarettes = painful, premature death

Get the picture? By playing this little game, you are facilitating your internal rewiring to abandon bad habits and create good ones.

Now, there are always objects in your environment that have you hardwired in ways you might not even be aware of. Things around you trigger certain behaviors or dynamics, good or bad.

Let's say you've been binge-eating late at night while sitting in a particular spot on your sofa watching TV. Now you've decided you really want to stop that behavior. But every time you sit in that spot on the sofa, you find it impossible to stop snacking. You cannot rationally "think" these kinds of ingrained habits away. They are wired into your brain with an actual physical, associative connection. But you can swap out old objects that trigger you negatively for new objects that trigger you positively. So in this example maybe you sell the sofa or give it to Goodwill and get a new seating arrangement that has no associations with midnight Doritos parties, allowing you to "turn over a new leaf." Or if you can't afford a new sofa, you slipcover it and use it to meditate, or you sit there to read a favorite author. Follow me? You want to create a positive association with sitting on that sofa instead of what you had before.

Here's another example. Many people who go through a breakup with someone buy new sheets. They associate the old bedsheets with the old person, and they want to "start over." Out with the old and all that. Same idea.

You can also form positive associations with seemingly random objects that give you psychological support. How many of you have a good luck charm? Every morning I make tea, and I have a large cup collection that I choose from. If I use my disappearing dinosaur cup one morning and on that day I am particularly successful in my work, I will reuse that damned cup until it crumbles in my clammy death grip or until my streak is broken.

A friend who shall go unnamed (so I don't embarrass the hell out of him) is a Major League Baseball player. His team had been on a losing streak, and then finally they won a game. My friend decided that the reason they won was that his son had given him a pair of "lucky socks" to wear for the game. He wore those socks for every game the entire season, and oddly enough, the team did pretty well. The socks, not so much. I only hope to God he was washing them between games.

You can see how it's possible, and sometimes even productive, to associate a certain dynamic with an object. My friend associated winning with his lucky socks. Obviously his socks do not have magic powers, but he believed they contributed to the team's success. So in a roundabout way, those socks contributed to his forming a habit of winning, by inciting a winning attitude and the behaviors that go along with it.

Now, don't get crazy and form some sort of emotional attachment to a teacup and some socks, or toss everything out of your home should you get dumped tomorrow. But there are ways you can use this physiological fact to alter your behavior.

One more example. Last for this chapter, promise.

If you want to lose weight and have been going to the same supermarket for years buying garbage foods, try a new supermarket! Find a local farmers' market with new grocers, new foods, in a new locale. Bring a good friend who shares and supports you and makes you laugh so you associate positive fun with that market. Start a new pattern of buying all healthy, nourishing foods. Then repeat!

On your road to success, you can harness this power of association to work for you in myriad ways. Your environment influences your thoughts, choices, and performance in life to a significantly deeper extent—that's why I've written a whole chapter about it. But before I get to environment in the macro sense, there's something I need to cover at a more basic level, and that is organization. If you want to be ready for the opportunities coming your way, you have to get your life in order, literally.

CHAPTER TEN

GET ORGANIZED

It's no good just floating through life expecting the things you want to fall out of the sky. A huge part of actually going after what you want proactively is organizing yourself to do so. There are two parts to it: organizing your goals and organizing your environment. (We'll deal with your environment in the larger sense in Chapter 11.) Organizing your goals is very simple and amazingly powerful—all you have to do is get out a pen and paper or sit down at your keyboard. The fact is, when we write down the things we want, we are way more likely to achieve them.

WRITE IT DOWN

The "mass of men" slog through life with no particular agenda, in a state of mind-numbing aimlessness. The average person sets generalized goals that simply focus on a positive outcome, such as "I want to be healthy" or "I want to be rich."

But the *exceptional* person is the one who knows what he or she wants and sets very specific goals that are not just about the outcome but about the process of getting there. This is why I talked early on about creating a powerful vision, so that you can define your goal in detail and dimension. Step Three underlines some of those lessons about goal-setting, but with a different focus: on action, not deliberation. We'll literally chart a road map of the steps you need to take to achieve your vision.

It starts with writing it down. A terrifying statistic floating around on the Internet says 95 percent of people don't have written goals and they fail because of it, while 5 percent do write down their goals, and they succeed. Who knows where these statistics come from, but in my experience, this one has to be pretty close to accurate. There are so many reasons why it's important to write your goals down. Lucky for you, I'm going to break them down one by one.

First, from a psychological perspective, seeing your goals in writing makes them more real and forces you to form an emotional attachment to them. They become concrete things instead of vague hopes floating around in the back of your mind.

From a practical standpoint, writing down your goals will help bring a direction and focus to your day so you don't waste energy or spin your wheels. Many people get caught in activity traps that waste time, thereby rendering themselves unproductive and increasingly discouraged. The trick is not to prioritize your schedule, but to schedule your priorities. Cliché number—well, who's counting?

Additionally, long-term goals can be overwhelming, and many people struggle to keep sight of the big picture. It's easy to become intimidated by the details and worry about everything you will have to do to get where you ultimately want to be. But if you let that happen, you will give up before you've even begun. So it's not just about getting your goal down on paper, but doing so in a very specific way. Break your goal down into bite-size steps so that you understand clearly just how manageable each one is, just how achievable your goal will be when you approach it appropriately.

The most effective way to begin is at the end. The end goal you have in mind is the frame of reference for everything you do. Be specific. Have a way to measure what you've done. And create goals that are achievable. They should also be challenging enough that they require at least six months to a year to accomplish. Be mindful of some common pitfalls:

Now, really? Unless you are six feet tall and dangerously skinny, you will probably never be a supermodel. But you can still take great care of yourself and look amazing and become an on-camera fashion correspondent, or work as an editor at a fashion magazine, become a stylist, what have you. There's always a way to find work in whatever world you love, even if it's not in the way you first think.

Don't be vague. Don't start out with a goal like "I want to be happy." You must define what happiness *means* to you before you can go out and achieve it. Does it mean being married to the man of your dreams and living on a ranch in Montana? Or does it mean living on Wall Street as the CEO of a Fortune 500 company?

What's your yardstick? Don't set a goal like "I want to be thin and healthy." My contestants and *Losing It* families say things like that all the time. But when I ask them what that actually means in real terms, they have no answer. If you don't have a clear idea of what something looks like, what something is, how will you know you've achieved it? Instead, try saying "I want my blood pressure at 120/80," or "I want to be able to run a half marathon," or "I want to lose 60 pounds."

Once you have determined the ultimate goal, make a plan for how to reach it using short-term goals. This is where you break it down to manageable stages, those bite-size pieces I discussed above.

One of the best ways to break the big 'uns into small, attainable short-term goals is to create a goal pyramid. It will allow you to literally plot a course of action, connecting the things you are doing right this moment to the future you envision for yourself. Your ultimate goal goes right at the top, followed underneath by monthly, then weekly, then daily, then even hourly goals.

WORKING IT OUT

Copy the blank chart on page 182 and get cracking. After you have filled it in, keep a copy with you at all times to remind yourself of what you need to do to keep on track. I have created an example here to help you get the idea.

Writing down tasks and organizing them by scale and time frame is an invaluable practical tool when it comes to achievement. Reviewing your goals regularly is a crucial part of your success, and must become part of your routine. Post copies of your pyramid in your office, on the fridge, on the bathroom mirror, by your bed—wherever you're going to see them regularly and often. Look at your goals throughout the day to focus yourself so that each day contributes in a meaningful way to your overall vision. Each morning when you wake up, look at the pyramid. Reevaluate your immediate and daily goals. Then each night, right before you go to bed, evaluate what you achieved and what remains to be accomplished. This process will keep both your subconscious and your conscious mind engaged and working toward fulfilling your aspirations.

This pyramid of goals will also help you build motivation and self-assurance. As you achieve some of the smaller goals, those successes will inspire confidence in your ability to do more. Don't forget, success begets success.

Another way to stay motivated is to reward yourself for knocking out the smaller goals. Now, let me be very clear: these rewards are to be life affirming, not self-destructive. In other words, if your goal is weight loss, you're not to give yourself a weekly reward of pizza with Coke and a sundae. Instead, get yourself a manicure and a pedicure. When you hit your monthly goals, maybe splurge

Goal Pyramid

LONG-TERM GOAL

MONTHLY GOALS

WEEKLY GOALS

DAILY GOALS

IMMEDIATE GOALS

Goal Pyramid Example

LONG-TERM GOAL 100-pound weight loss

MONTHLY GOALS Drop 12 pounds

(Monthly goals will equal what you realistically need to lose to hit this target in under a year, and the same applies for breaking it down further to weekly, daily, and immediate goals.)

WEEKLY GOALS
Lose 3 pounds.
Hit the gym 5 times
for 45 minutes each session.
Maintain a weekly calorie allowance
of roughly 8,500 calories.

DAILY GOALS
MONDAY: Hit the gym. Reconcile my food
journal at the end of the day to make sure I am
at my 1,200 daily calorie allowance.
TUESDAY: Hit the gym. Write in my food journal
to make sure I am at my daily calorie allowance.
WEDNESDAY: Go grocery shopping for healthy groceries
to cook and pack. Watch my journal to make sure I am at my
1,200 daily calorie allowance.
THURSDAY: Hit the gym. Reconcile my food journal at the
end of the day. Cook food for the week so I have healthy
meals prepared at all times.
FRIDAY: Buy new workout clothes. Hit the gym. Stay on top of my
food journal.
SATURDAY: Work out and maintain my food journal.
SUNDAY: Plan my schedule for the week so I make time in each day for my
workouts, also to make time to buy and cook healthy groceries. Wash and
clean my gym clothes and gym bag.

*(Next, move on to immediate goals, or what you need to do moment to moment
to facilitate your daily goals.)*

IMMEDIATE GOALS
Buy a calorie counter that I can carry with me. Call the other moms at school
to see if they can carpool with me so I can squeeze a workout in several mornings a week.
Look up a few healthy recipes online, so I know what healthy groceries to buy for this
week's healthy meal preparation. Print out my gym schedule so I have it for Sunday when
I plan my weekly workouts.

on a massage. When you hit your long-term goal, maybe indulge in a beach vacation or a new wardrobe.

Giving yourself these healthy treats is also a great way to learn how to be more loving to yourself. So few of us take the time to be good to ourselves in the right ways. Scheduling these kinds of nurturing activities so that they correspond to achieving your goals will do wonders for your self-esteem and help you cultivate a healthy outlook on life.

I used to struggle with this issue personally for years. I felt that pampering myself was indulgent, excessive, and self-serving. I told you I had issues from childhood, remember? Anyway, one day I was in therapy and was feeling particularly lonely and empty. I was complaining about how I do everything for everyone else and no one does anything for me. Then my shrink, in all his wisdom, shined a light—aka dropped the smackdown—and once again changed my life. "It's not other people you resent. It's you. You are giving all the things you desire to other people. You buy them flowers and presents. You get them massages. You take them out for a night on the town, but you never do these things for yourself, and you wonder why you feel unfulfilled. When you give yourself these things and treat yourself in this nurturing way, you won't feel a lack in your life, and what everyone else contributes will be an exciting bonus." In addition, he pointed out that I expected people to read my mind 'cause I was too insecure to ask for what I wanted, and so I also needed to work on clearly expressing my needs—which we will cover in Chapter 12.

I digress, but regardless, pampering yourself and rewarding yourself through nurturing incentives can go a long way in helping you achieve not only your goals but also fulfillment in your life overall.

Once you have your goals organized, the next step is to organize your life. Literally. The best way to facilitate your goal pyramid is to make sure you have the ordered mental and physical space to do so.

CLEAR THE DECKS

This is about as self-explanatory and straightforward as it gets. You don't necessarily have to become neater, cleaner, or more punctual, although those things certainly don't suck. Rather, you need to arrange the things in your life so that you are ready for all the great opportunities life has to offer.

Disorganization hampers us by creating chaos in our lives and obstacles that make it difficult for us to jump at opportunities when they come along. Keeping your environment at home and at work organized can benefit your mental and physical health in any number of ways.

It's essential for time management, because it allows you to do and accomplish more in your day. Think about it: how many times have you been late to something because you couldn't find your keys, your wallet, or the shirt that went with your outfit? Chaos costs you time that you can't afford to lose. If you live in disarray, doing simple chores like paying bills and cleaning the house is going to take you at least twice as long. Without a system you likely won't be able to find the tools you need for the task at hand.

Honestly, how much time do you waste by being scattered? Think of *all* the things you could do with that time! You could hit the gym, squeeze in some extra sleep, spend a little quality time playing with your kid, get to work early and pull down some overtime to save up for that vacation . . . and on and on.

Studies have shown that people who live in a cluttered environment show mental signs of distraction and are quicker to become overwhelmed and stressed. By streamlining your life, you streamline your thoughts and become able to focus your energies in a more proactive, effective way.

Organization also enhances self-esteem. How you keep your living environment is a direct reflection of your relationship with yourself. For example, how you keep your kitchen is a clue about whether you are giving proper attention to your own nourishment. When we were shooting *Losing It,* invariably every family whose home I invaded had a filthy fridge, overstuffed with food to the point that much of it had gone bad and the family didn't even notice. The shelves would be sticky with old soda. The vegetables would be shoved in a bottom drawer covered in mold. The pantry would be overflowing with processed garbage that had been opened, spilled, and left unsealed. In some cases mice were *nesting* in the cupboards.

These were people whose physical health was in a total state of ruin, which was evident just by the way they cared for, or didn't care for, their kitchens. The same thing goes for every other area of your home, your workspace, or wherever you spend time; you have power over your surroundings.

The reverse is true, too—your surroundings have power over you. When your office is a mess, you are often distracted and unproductive at work. When your bathroom is a mess, you are most likely neglecting your hygiene. I could go on. By keeping your life and your surroundings organized and well looked after, you are making a statement that you value yourself, a statement that reaffirms itself to you whenever you look around.

And last but not least, by clearing things out and organizing your life, you are declaring yourself ready to let go of all the superfluous crap you've been needlessly hanging on to and ready to be open to new possibilities. Every magazine and piece of paper you recycle, every book you give to the library, and every knick-knack and item of clothing you release to a new owner creates space in your life for new insight, energy, joy, and experiences to come in! It is amazing to witness the transformations and the freedom that you gain by being organized.

If organization is a particular problem for you, take a good, honest look at your life and ask yourself what being disorganized is costing you in terms of achievement, productivity, health, relationships, and self-esteem. Your answers may help motivate you to make changes. Stop thinking of clutter-clearing as some tremendous chore, and start thinking of it as one of the most effective self-improvement tactics at your disposal.

Here are a few tricks and exercises to get you on track:

Schedule time to de-clutter. Put in fifteen minutes every day to straighten up. Do your dishes, make your bed, put your clothes in the laundry, and so on. By breaking this stuff down into small daily tasks, you won't be overwhelmed with a huge mess by week's end.

Set an example. If you have a family, lead by example and use positive incentives with your kids. Many parents (moms in particular) get overwhelmed when trying to wrangle the family to keep things clean and tidy. Although draconian measures might seem like your only option, they seldom work and will leave you feeling even more depleted and defeated. Your best bet is to set the tone for your family by keeping yourself organized. Then you can establish some positive incentives, like offering them a small allowance or the privilege of an extracurricular activity like cheerleading or hockey if they keep their rooms clean, take out the trash, or wash the dishes. Kids crave structure, and giving them healthy boundaries allows them to feel secure and helps prepare them for the real world. Once you establish these ground rules, be sure to remain firm in your resolve. If you backtrack, you jeopardize your authority and your ability to maintain the rules of your house.

File it away. Make an action file, to sort all the different paperwork in your life. Each day sort mail and other paper into the appropriately labeled file. Have slots for bills to pay, appointments to make, errands to run, and things to concentrate on at work or at home—the different elements that your life contains. Then take ten minutes over the weekend to manage the business that came in over the past week so you can jump into the new week with a clean slate and no unresolved issues nagging at you.

Don't forget your pyramid. Create a daily to-do list from your goal pyramid. This will help you prioritize your time. At the beginning of the day or before you go to bed each night, take a moment to think about what you need to accomplish immediately in order to move your life forward and get closer to your long-term goal. These little actions in the present can lead to big results in the future.

Time to be smart. Be smart and manage your time properly. Don't be afraid to ask for help or to delegate chores to loved ones or coworkers. A smart person knows they can't do it all and has the ego strength to reach out when necessary. When you want to squeeze in a workout, try asking your friends and family to watch the kids. Instead of resorting to the drive-through, take turns with your spouse so that one of you can watch the kids while the other prepares a healthy meal.

You might have everything organized and planned out to a T, but unconscious actions can creep in and erode even the best intentions. Which is why it's crucial to create an environment that is geared as much as possible toward your success. And that's what the next chapter is all about.

CHAPTER ELEVEN

CREATE THE RIGHT ENVIRONMENT

One thing that is paramount to your success is gaining some control over your immediate surroundings. Ever heard the saying, "You are a product of your environment?" Cliché? Perhaps. True? Hell, yes!

So you need to create an environment that will promote vital behaviors rather than self-destructive ones. Yes, there are a whole lot of things about the world you can't change. But in your immediate, personal environment, it's a different story. We all actually have a lot of power over our surroundings. While you can't single-handedly stop pollution and heal the planet, for example, you *can* install an air purifier in your house, use natural cleaning products, install energy-efficient lightbulbs, and generally green up your home and lifestyle.

You can learn how to use your proactive focus to manipulate the aspects of your environment that you *do* have power over, so that your surroundings are geared as much as possible toward helping rather than hindering your efforts.

There are two parts to your environment: things and people. Obviously, you can control things, but you can't *control* people. Dealing with people falls largely under the umbrella of communication, which I'll get to in Chapter 12. So let's start with things, by far the easier part of your environment—not only do things not talk back, but once you change them, they generally stay changed. So what kind of changes am I talking about?

Whether it's objects, space, sights, sounds, or smells, everything around you sends you messages and affects your thoughts and behavior. Environmental things, cues, and conditions can sabotage you or support you. So how do you create a supportive environment? It takes two simple actions: attending and pruning.

ATTENTION!

More often than not, powerful influences in our environment are invisible to us. This lack of awareness can destroy our good intentions. Unknown to us, these environmental cues can affect our thoughts and behaviors. Work procedures, office layouts, checkout counters at supermarkets, vending machines in schools, super-size meals, commercials on TV, supermodels on every magazine cover and in every ad, and so on—these things have a dramatic effect on what we think and what we do, yet we may fail to recognize the potency of their influence.

So your first order of business is to look around your environment and identify the things there that trip you up. Be deliberate in your search; if it's weight you struggle with, look for things that trigger you to eat. If it's money issues, look for things that trigger you to spend. You get the idea. When you sweep the field for these sabotaging items, make sure you include your home, mode of transport, and place of business—anywhere and everywhere you spend time on a regular or semiregular basis. Here's the list I made of things at work that sabotage my diet:

Craft service and catering for production crew
Coffee truck loaded with doughnuts, cookies, and pastries
Food commercials on TV while I'm in hair and makeup

WORKING IT OUT

Now it's your turn. Take some time, and make a list of all the things in your daily life that have the potential to set you back or do you damage in any way. Remember, be thorough!

Things that sabotage me at home:

Things that sabotage me at work:

Things that sabotage me in general:

BRING IN A SUBSTITUTE

Once you have identified as many sources of sabotage as you can, the next step is to see if you can find a way to remove, replace, or circumvent them. Your goal is to get these things out of the way, so you don't have to rely on willpower alone to keep yourself on track. Willpower, like a muscle, gets fatigued and can sometimes crap out on us when we most need it. I'll talk about strategies for building and strengthening your willpower in Chapter 13, but in general you should always leave it as untested as possible. All you need to reduce your risk of running into trouble is a little creative planning and forethought.

Obviously there are some sabotaging elements that you can't just remove—that vending machine at the office, for example. But there *are* proactive ways to combat it. Nip temptation in the bud by buying a mini-fridge and popping it next to your desk, then stocking it with healthy snacks so you're not tempted to go for the processed stuff. If you can avoid walking past that damned machine by taking different routes around the office, do it!

If the fashion magazines and websites you look at make you feel bad about yourself, stop bringing them into your home and your life! Instead read something inspirational that motivates you, like *this book*. If you're in debt and struggling to get out, bypass going to the mall and instead buy the thing you need online to avoid further temptation. It's kind of like baby-proofing a house—you look for the trouble spots and try to eliminate them or reduce their power to take you down.

Here are my solutions to the sabotaging elements I'm exposed to at work that could disrupt my healthy diet:

Problem: Craft service and catering for production crew

Solution: Though it's the quickest route, I don't *have* to walk past the craft service area to get to the gym or the house on *Biggest Loser*. I can take the extra five minutes and go the long way, removing temptation from the equation entirely.

Problem: Coffee truck loaded with doughnuts, cookies, and pastries

Solution: This one's tough, because I'm not about to go without caffeine. But I can avoid the coffee truck and the pastry buffet entirely and keep a coffeemaker in my dressing room.

Problem: Food commercials on TV while I'm in hair and makeup

Solution: I can simply turn off the TV and listen to music instead, which has the opposite effect and makes me want to work out rather than eat. At home I can TiVo all the shows I want to watch and fast-forward through all the food commercials that tempt me.

By such techniques you can alter your environment to eliminate choice entirely, leaving less room for error and slipups. It doesn't require much work either, just a little planning and small changes in behavior.

Seek out the high-voltage areas of your life, and find resourceful ways of avoiding them. This will help you preserve your willpower for times you simply can't stay out of harm's way. Remember, willpower is like a muscle—you can build it up and strengthen it, but the more you use it without a break, the more fatigued it gets. For most of us, willpower is usually a fleeting burst of strength and bravado. It's the moment where I choose not to walk out the back door past the craft service table and use the front door instead. It's the moment when you ask the waiter not to bring bread to the table. It's that moment when your better judgment takes over before your willpower can be worn down. But when we are constantly exposed to temptation, ultimately willpower wears thin, even for the most determined.

The takeaway: you can't get into trouble if trouble isn't there to get into! The more you remove potential trouble spots from your surroundings, or build barriers against them by planning ahead, the less likely you are to be thrown off course or deflected from your goal.

You can and should take it one step further by not just removing troublesome instigators but also replacing them with positive influences. The more you surround yourself with stimuli that motivate and empower you, the more you will be motivated and empowered. Simple, right? This goes for *everything* around you. Give your entire environment, including the media you are digesting, an overhaul: the books and magazines you're reading, the TV shows you're watching, the music you listen to, the websites you frequent, the route you take to work, the food in your cupboards, the art on your walls, and on and on.

If you are spending too much money, turn off the Home Shopping Network and TiVo some Suze Orman so she can give you a little money-saving pep talk. Move the elliptical machine that has been collecting dust in your basement up to your living room so you can use it while hanging out with your family or watching TV. If the street vendors in the subway station tempt you on your way to work, be sure to always eat a healthy breakfast beforehand and chew gum so that the thought of mixing gum and fattening street food puts you off.

WORKING IT OUT

Now it's your turn again.

For every object in your environment that has the potential to sabotage you, come up with something you can replace it with or a behavior you can counteract it with. Things don't talk back or resist change or have an agenda of their own; once you change them, they stay changed. Alas, people? Not so much.

THE COMPANY YOU KEEP

Sociologists have done countless studies on how physical space and proximity play into our behaviors and relationships. Now that we've seen how the things in our immediate surroundings have a dramatic impact on us, let's look at our dynamics with the people around us. You can get physically close to someone in order to foster a relationship, build your circle of influence, gain an ally, learn something new, strengthen your network of support, and so on. Let me give you an example.

On *Biggest Loser* there's always at least one contestant who's very focused and determined, and there's always one who's not. I'll train them together, put them side by side on treadmills, and make them room next to each other. In almost every case the less focused contestant rises to the occasion and takes on the determined characteristics of the stronger contestant. I have also taken contestants who disliked each other at the outset, trained them together, and watched them become fast friends. I was able to implement a support system for them while simultaneously eliminating excess animosity and tension from the *Biggest Loser* house. This worked because the frequency and quality of human interaction is largely based on physical proximity. The reverse is also true: create space between people, and they tend to become estranged.

It's time for one of my favorite clichés: "You are the company you keep." This one's a cliché for good reason. Research shows that we adopt many behaviors from our peers. It's just basic human nature. We want the people we hang with to like us, so we unconsciously take on their behaviors, habits, and mannerisms. You know where this is going, right?

If you hang out with positive people, they will have a positive influence on you. If you hang around with burnouts, they will have a negative influence on you. I've seen countless articles on this behavior, how your friends and family can affect everything from your weight to your finances. Hell, that's what *Losing It* was all about—families who had, together, become so unhealthy that their lives were at risk. The people around us set the standards for our behavior, and we fall in line. Even if you grew up being taught to value independence and autonomy, this instinct to fit in and adapt to our surroundings is a basic human drive.

Here's a personal anecdote to illustrate what I'm talking about. When I was a kid going through my parents' divorce, I hung out with other troubled teens who were skipping school, experimenting with drugs and alcohol, and getting into trouble wherever they could find it. Naturally I followed suit. My grades plummeted, I started shoplifting, and at the ripe old age of thirteen I hit my heaviest weight: 175 pounds. It wasn't pretty.

Thank God my mama stepped in and took action to straighten me out. She's the one who got me into martial arts, which as you know turned my life around. My teacher and the other students in the dojo were healthy, focused, motivated individuals who wanted to excel in their lives personally, professionally, and physically. Among these people, drinking, eating crap, and failing out of school were shockingly uncool. I admired the students and my teacher and wanted to be like them. As a result, my behaviors, habits, and outlook all changed for the better. You know how it ended: I got thin and healthy, went on to have a successful career, and am living happily ever after.

This social mimicry most often happens without our even realizing it. I'm now a strong-minded, outspoken thirty-six-year-old woman, and I *still* find myself falling into this pattern. My *Biggest Loser* cohort Bob Harper and I were total opposites when we met. He was Mr. Fashion, I was Ms. Jeans & T-shirt. I loved motorcycles and fast cars, and he was terrified of them. Now we're like twins! He got me into fashion, and we even wear a lot of the same designers. I got him into motorcycles, and now he proudly rides around L.A. on his Ducati 1198S. We find ourselves speaking alike, using similar hand gestures. One morning I even woke up with his horrible laugh: *Hunh-hunh-hunh.* (And in case you're wondering, no, I still haven't shaken it—can someone please shoot me?) We've changed each other simply because of the fact that we spend *so much* time together.

UNDER THE INFLUENCE

Let's look at an example on a different scale. Silicon Valley, California, has produced more entrepreneurial companies than any other American city in recent decades. Is it because there's something in the water supply? No! It's because individuals who have been close to and learned from their coworkers or bosses then go on to start their own successful companies, and a domino effect takes place, and still others follow suit. Monkey see, monkey do. In this particular instance the influence was good, but it can also work in the reverse.

This dynamic exists at every level of human interaction, whether it's among family members, colleagues, friends, or fellow churchgoers—basically anywhere you have more than one person sharing space. And it's an extremely valuable tool in human interaction. So how do we use it to our advantage?

Easy. If there is a person you are interested in, someone who you think can teach you something or help you in some way, put yourself in their orbit. Go to the same gym they do. Sit next to them at the cafeteria. Hang out with the same friends. Join the same clubs. Basically get up in their grill.

Conversely, if there is someone around you who has a detrimental effect on you, put as much space between you and them as possible. You may feel daunted at the prospect of kicking assholes out of your life, but it's really quite simple. By removing yourself from their space, you take away their ability to affect you.

Remove yourself physically from places you know they will be. If they commute on the same train as you, take the bus. Avoid the restaurants or bars they frequent. If you're stationed next to them at work, swap offices with another coworker to gain space, or consider a job change. I've known people who have moved to a different city to get away from an unhealthy relationship. With any luck you won't have to go to such extremes. But in "pursuit of happiness," it is imperative that you remove unhappy, discouraging, or destructive dynamics from your world.

Although traditionally this applies to physical space, cyberspace has become equally as real and impactful, so you must remove them from those means of contact as well. "Defriend" them on Facebook. Change your e-mail address. Protect your tweets. Block them on AOL Messenger. Change your phone number.

The bottom line is that savvy, ambitious people know how to use physical space and proximity with others to their advantage. They use it to enhance interaction with influential people and get to a point of collaboration, and to distance themselves from negative influences at all costs. (Okay, not *all* costs. I guess I would draw the line at, you know, murder. Though I sure am tempted sometimes . . .)

GET A LITTLE CLOSER

You're probably wondering *how* to get closer to people you admire or want to learn from. Let's be honest—there's a fine line between striking up a learning relationship with someone and stalking them. The key to keeping this productive (and legal) is your intentions and your actions when you meet the person. Your goal is to gain access, make a good impression, and ultimately build your system of learning and support. There are a number of ways you can interact with people you want to get to know. Maybe they belong to clubs, maybe they take part in certain activities, maybe they socialize with a certain set in certain places, maybe you can friend them on Facebook—in this day and age the possibilities are endless.

I got to know Suze Orman this way. I'd always admired her, and I'd gotten to a point in my career where I really wanted to meet her, pick her brain, get her feedback and advice. Having built a super brand with integrity and purpose, she'd done with money and finance what I wanted to do with health and wellness. So Giancarlo and I looked on her website and noted down every single one of her speaking engagements for the entire year. He then started calling these places and offering to have me speak for free. I didn't want payment, I just wanted to get close enough to meet her and strike up a conversation. It worked, sort of.

As I mentioned earlier, the conference where we were both scheduled to speak was canceled, but we bonded over that, and the rest is, as they say, history. She took me under her wing and has been invaluable in helping me advance my career and get my message of health and empowerment to a wider audience.

See? Meeting the people you want to meet and building your social network is not that hard. Can it be scary? Definitely! I realize that it can. We all fear rejection, we all have egos, so this step can be very challenging. That said, it's time to suck it up. (Sorry, but it is.) If a person rejects you, it won't result in death. A little bruising to the ego maybe, but no one can hurt your feelings unless you let them. Ultimately, if someone rejects you, you can look at it as doing you a favor. Remember, "rejection is God's protection" (cliché number 1,578). They've shown you who they are, so you can move on and find a better fit.

Getting close to someone is, of course, only half the battle. Once you get close, what do you *do* with that proximity? You know how quickly you form an opinion of someone. Be honest, you know, or you think you know, within minutes whether you like someone's vibe, whether they are polite, and whether they are to be taken seriously or not.

I can speak personally from both sides of the equation. Not only have I sought people out to help me advance and develop, but also now that I'm successful in my field, young trainers seek me out, hoping for advice on how to build their business or improve their craft. Now, I'm not exactly a tough person to engage. You can communicate with me on my website, follow me on Twitter, go to one of my speaking engagements around the country, and so on. It's easy enough to meet me, but I can't help every trainer in the business, so the people who make an impression on me are the ones who have done their homework. They've educated themselves about me and my philosophies, so they're able to open a dialogue that engages me, which leads to a natural furthering of the relationship.

This is how Brett Hoebel became the new male trainer on

Biggest Loser for season eleven. He got in my space and really impressed me. He was talented, passionate, and articulate, and he'd done his homework. I began taking capoeira lessons from him, and when the time came for the show to cast some new blood, I lobbied passionately for him to get the job.

QUIZ
Are You
Ready to
Live an
Exceptional
Life?

Before you gain access to someone who can help you, you will need to have mastered some of the basics of high-level communication. Powerful, effective communication is one of the best weapons in your arsenal. I'll give you three guesses what we're going to talk about next.

CHAPTER TWELVE

MASTER COMMUNICATION

FIRST RULE: PLAY WELL WITH OTHERS

Most of us spend the majority of our waking hours interacting with other human beings, talking to or listening to them, working with or next to them . . . you get the picture. So it's pretty much guaranteed that other people are going to play a role in your success or failure. Your ability to talk and listen *well*, not only to communicate but also to cooperate and collaborate with others, is just as important as all that personal growth and emotional development we talked about in Steps One and Two.

Eleanor Roosevelt, one of my heroes (in case you hadn't figured that out), put it beautifully: "Nobody ever really does anything alone. For every achievement in life it's essential to deal with other people." In other words, no man, no woman, is an island. And who the hell would want to be? Interaction with others is how we grow and develop, both personally and professionally.

Professionally, communication skills are *crucial*. You can't succeed in a vacuum. The most successful people in the world are those who understand the power of social capital, which is really just a fancy term for networking. You can't achieve anything if you don't risk anything, and when taking a risk, it helps to be able to draw on a network of support to minimize that risk. Building social capital is key to almost any professional scenario you can imagine. It's what you know *and* who you know that bridge the difference between success or failure. But how do you build that all-important capital? And why is it so important? Let's take a look.

Having good social capital helps you:

Learn the ropes. If you are new in a job or have recently moved up or to a new position, you're going to want to jump in and hit the ground running. So you're going to need to reach out to more experienced colleagues to help you figure out how things work.

Expand your business. Connections in business are critical, whichever business you're talking about. In order to expand that business, you have to be able to attract people, draw them to you. Strong communication skills will allow you to court potential business partners with grace and aptitude.

Climb the ladder. If you want to be first in line for a promotion, you need to impress and earn the respect of your boss. Doing good work and having good ideas is essential, but on their own they're not going to propel you to the top. The impressions you give off to others will be key. You need to be a strong advocate for yourself by communicating your good ideas in a way that guarantees they'll be heard. Do your homework so you can speak up intelligently in meetings. Listen to the feedback you get so you can incorporate it and improve your game. Communication—both talking and listening—is going to help you put your best foot forward every time.

Improve customer service. If you have your own business, then you know that companies live and die by their customer service. Listening to the wants, needs, frustrations, and aspirations of your customers is the golden rule of most any endeavor, retail or otherwise. By the same token, you also have to be able to sell your product, which means communicating in a convincing and trust-worthy manner. Connecting with your customer in these ways will set your business apart from the rest.

Avoid blind spots. In business, knowledge gives advantage, and often what you don't know can sink you before your ship even sets sail. Since you obviously can't know *everything*, it helps to align yourself with people who may know more than you or have different areas of expertise. One of the keys to my success so far has been surrounding myself with people who are smarter than me. I'm serious. I did this with my business partner, Giancarlo. He fills in all my blind spots and helps me avoid pitfalls. I would be nowhere today had I not surrounded myself with smart, creative, talented people. They all enhanced the quality and integrity of our (Giancarlo's and my) company. There's only one catch: to recruit this kind of support, you need to check your ego at the door and cultivate a true team mentality by being willing to listen to and collaborate with others.

Do I need to go on? If you plan on succeeding, you should have a network of people you can turn to for expertise, as well as a network for support. Period. And to build them you need to master the fine art of communication. And it doesn't stop with business.

In our personal lives, the same principles of collaboration and effective communication are vital to maintaining strong and healthy relationships with friends, family, significant others— basically anyone who shares your life in any capacity at all. Here are some examples of how essential communication skills are to helping us avoid pitfalls and to improving the overall quality of our lives. They help us:

Disable enablers. Often, when we look closely, we will find that some of the people around us are contributing to our problems by taking on the role of enabler or disabler.

When I was shooting *Losing It,* I would see families constantly playing out this dynamic of enabling and disabling. One family member would start losing weight, then another would feel threatened by that and attempt to sabotage their progress. It's not necessarily conscious or malicious, but it has a negative effect anyway. Knowing how to communicate your concerns, your needs, and your dreams, to cocreate solutions and move through conflict, is vital to the health and happiness of your relationships.

Manage misunderstandings. Misunderstandings are toxic, especially in your personal relationships. Conveying your message to others clearly and without judgment while receiving the information you are given is key to maintaining harmony and equality in your relationships. I can't tell you how many times someone has misconstrued something I've said, written, or done, thinking that I was angry or upset when really I was just kidding around with good intentions.

We are all different! We don't think or behave alike. And this is a beautiful thing. That said, it means you have to keep your communication as unambiguous as possible. Express how you are feeling clearly—don't let things fester or resentment build. You can help the other person do the right thing by telling them how you feel and what you need. Conversely, if someone is telling you how *they* feel, listen with an open heart and try not to be judgmental or defensive. This allows you insight into the other person and how best to get along with them.

Become better at compromise. People disagree all the time. It's part of life. But as a result, so is negotiation to reach a healthy compromise. Whether our disagreements are small or huge, over time they can wear on any relationship, unless we handle them with diplomacy, patience, and a spirit of compromise. You know exactly what I'm talking about. He wants Mexican, and you want sushi. He wants to go to Vegas for a romantic weekend getaway, while you want to go to Cabo. He thinks the kids should be in public school, you want them in private. Navigating these kinds of issues is impossible without strong communication skills. Life is not about winning or losing—it's about developing the ability to find solutions. And communication is what's going to get you there.

SIGN OF STRENGTH

These are just a few examples of how essential communication skills are in our lives. For those of you who get it, great—skip ahead to "Listen Up." For those of you who feel it's weak to express your needs and feelings, or that you don't need any help, get over it and stop being an idiot.

Expressing your feelings and being vulnerable are signs of strength. Another one of my favorite quotes says it perfectly: "You can only know as much happiness and joy as you can know vulnerability." It's from Kahlil Gibran's *The Prophet*—again. Can you tell I love that book?

Think about it. Seriously. If you don't ask for the promotion, someone else will, and they'll probably get it because they've spoken openly and honestly about their ambition. If you don't tell your significant other when something hurts your feelings, the silence will erode your relationship over time, and resentment will spread its poison, until what was once a small grievance becomes something much bigger. If you don't ask for it, you won't get it. And if you don't talk about the problem, it won't get resolved. Nothing ventured, nothing gained. So all right already: speak up!

We *all* need help from time to time, and those of us who feel worthy and secure enough to ask for it are the ones who will reap the spoils. People who don't ask for help, or who fear letting others in on collaborative efforts, may do so for many reasons, ranging from self-esteem issues to ego. Here's the bottom line: if you can't communicate with other people, you're fucked. Sorry for the foul language, but if you meet this description, you needed to hear it, and now you need to go back to Step Two and work on whatever it is that's holding you back.

Enough digression. Now, it's time to learn a thing or two about successful communication. The tools that follow will help you perfect the art of communication with other people so that your life is smoother and more peaceful and you feel more fulfilled. We'll work on listening, speaking, and negotiating, and other basics of human interaction along the way.

Communication is, obviously, a two-way street. So I'm breaking this next section down into two topics: listening and speaking.

LISTEN UP!

Listening is the foundation of any productive conversation. A conversation is kind of like a dance. It requires a flow of interaction, a rhythm of give-and-take, a balance of expression and understanding. Often we can be so intent on getting our point across that we forget we need to listen. And I'm not just talking about shutting up for a second. I'm talking about listening, not just with the intent to reply but with the intent to truly understand.

It's easy to fall into a pattern of projecting our own issues and experiences onto other people's words. We read into things people say based on our own inner dialogue, and we try to figure them out based on what we know of our own motives. We reply and give advice based on our own frame of reference, but that isn't necessarily what's called for in every situation. Unless we are really listening, our conversations can turn into nothing more than two people giving speeches as opposed to creating dialogue.

I was invited to appear on the *Dr. Phil* show once. The topic was "The Fat Debate." The National Association to Advance Fat Acceptance, a group of obese people who were aiming to stop discrimination against fat people, were fighting for "society" to make certain concessions based on their weight. So the "fat panel," comprising three obese women, was one side of the debate. I was on the "fit panel" along with another trainer wearing a T-shirt that said "No Chubbies." (I'm totally, 100 percent serious.) His mother had been overweight and blamed him his entire life for making her gain weight during pregnancy. The third person on our side was a nutritionist whose entire family had died of obesity-related disease. The show went down pretty badly. Every time the obese ladies would speak, the other trainer and the nutritionist would wait for them to finish, then pounce on them, attacking them for being lazy, judging them for making excuses, and so on.

This led the fat panel to become defensive and distrustful of the motives behind the advice being given to them, and they couldn't accept it. What they wanted and needed was to be treated with respect. They weren't saying they were healthy, but they *were* trying to explain that they were engaged in lifelong struggles, and that the cultural judgment and discrimination they experienced only made it worse.

The other two on my panel weren't able to hear that because they were too busy unconsciously projecting their own rage and hurt onto the women on the panel. Sadly, this meant that there was no resolution, and no one was helped. Those ladies needed help and could have been open to change, but the fit panel mentors weren't able to really listen and so weren't able to understand where they were coming from. Afterward, I was fortunate to make a connection with the ladies and actually went on to help one of them work on getting healthy.

One reason listening is so important is that everyone looks at the world through different eyes. Our different cultural backgrounds and life experiences have shaped the way we think and feel. Some of us come from a scarcity mentality, which drives us a certain way. Others come from an abundance mentality, which motivates us another way. Some of us believe in God, some of us don't. Republicans, Democrats—the examples of how different we all are from one another could make a book by themselves.

The point is, transcending the limits of our individual perceptions is critical to reaching a higher level of communication and thus a dramatically enhanced quality of life.

What we're aiming for is what many self-help gurus have labeled *empathic listening*. This is the kind of listening that puts you in the other person's head and in *their* frame of reference, so you truly get what they're feeling and understand what they're saying. Listening this way has two major benefits. First, you gain trust and greater openness, which is always going to lead to more possibilities for connection, resolution, and creativity. Second, you are getting exact information about what's going on, rather than just projecting your issues onto everything and everyone around you and acting on assumptions. And "when you assume something, it makes an ass out of you and me." (I couldn't help myself—it was right there, I had to say it.) Moving on to the bottom line, empathic listening allows you to create true and lasting communication and resolution.

It sounds great—but how do you listen empathically? It's not something that comes easily. You can't just decide you're going to be a better listener, and *bam*, you are. We're programmed at the deepest level to think with our ego, and overriding it takes awareness, desire, strength, and daring. Like almost everything, highly effective listening is a skill that you can work on and get better at with practice. This is a perfect opportunity for you to implement the techniques we discussed in Chapter 9—educate yourself on the subject, and build up your skill through target practice. Let's get started.

STAY PRESENT

This has got to be the tenth time I've told you to be aware and stay in the moment. Are you starting to see why it's so important not to check out? When you are listening to someone, make sure they know you are really listening. Stop what you are doing, look them in the eye, and give them your undivided attention. That means no checking your e-mail or phone, no TV, no multitasking—just focus on the words coming out of the other person's mouth.

BE AWARE OF WHAT YOUR BODY SAYS

Our body language plays a big part in what we communicate to the world. The way we carry ourselves gives clues to our purpose, intentions, and attitudes. Gestures, facial expressions, and posture all say a lot about what we're thinking and where we're coming from. Scientists say that nonverbal communication, as they call it, is often more essential to understanding than words themselves. Using body language gives you an advantage on two counts: you can read other people better, and you can get your message across better.

I can usually tell right away if someone is interested in me by the way they look at me, or how they carry themselves when talking to me. For example, if their arms are crossed, they may be angry or upset or feel threatened. So I'll give them a little space and make efforts not to be intrusive with my own body language or positioning. Or maybe they're looking at the ground regularly while talking to me. That could mean they're feeling intimidated, so I dial it down a little and take a step back. Paying attention to other people's body language gives you insight into how they're feeling, so you can adjust the way you're communicating.

Be conscious of how you're carrying yourself and how you're coming across. Are you smiling? Believe it or not, smiling is actually a powerful, *powerful* tool that puts people at ease and engenders instant positive feelings. Are your arms uncrossed, and is your posture open? This invites conversation and interaction. Are you maintaining eye contact? You know as well as I do that someone who can't look you in the eye is avoiding something and definitely looks a little shady. (But don't take someone's ability to look you in the eye as meaning they're honest: some of the best liars can do so with no problem.) Small gestures make a big difference in how you are perceived and can go a long way in conveying authenticity and interest. If you want to learn more about body language, there are some great books, including Janine Driver's *You Say More Than You Think* and Barbara and Allan Pease's *The Definitive Book of Body Language*.

FEEL THEIR PAIN

Empathic listening is about more than just hearing the words— it's about listening with the heart. Put yourself in the other person's shoes. Pay close attention to how the subject of discussion makes them feel. Take into consideration their different customs, values, and background. To get the full meaning of what they are trying to convey, you want to comprehend beyond just their words and your own personal frame of reference. Until you truly feel in your heart what it would be like to live through the same experience, you can never truly understand the other person. Once a person feels that you hear and understand them, you will have a tremendous amount of credibility and validity with them, which you can then use to move forward in a mutually beneficial direction.

This step can be more challenging than it sounds. There are all kinds of people in this world, and many of them are going to have values you disagree with, perhaps violently. Some of them are going to hold beliefs that offend you, often deeply. But we are all human, one tribe. And we can always *try* to find common ground. You do this with your heart, not with your head.

What do I mean? Just so you get the idea of how this can work in real life, here are some examples of difficult scenarios and possible commonalities. If you have religious differences, maybe a common ground is that you both love and believe in God. If you have political differences, perhaps you can find common ground in the fact that you both feel passionately about making the world a better place. Once you find these emotional intersections, you can begin to grasp where the other person is coming from. And from this jumping-off point you'll be able to move forward in a way that serves both of you. I'm so sick of telling you it won't be easy, but it won't. As I told you, I won't make you false promises, but I will provide you with answers and solutions. And if you want big things for yourself, you're going to have to figure this one out. FYI, I work on empathic listening *every day,* sometimes more successfully than others. It will get easier in time as you begin to see the benefits of your trials and tribulations.

LET THEM KNOW YOU LISTENED AND HEARD

Make sure your response lets the other person know they have been heard. You can listen empathically till you're blue in the face, but it won't do you much good unless the other person *knows* you're listening. Think about how you feel when you pour your heart out to someone, and as soon as they open their mouth, you see they haven't really heard a word you've said. It's frustrating, embarrassing, and hurtful as hell, right? Now think about how you feel when you can tell from someone's response that they get what you're saying. I bet you feel relieved, validated, comfortable, and open to hearing their point of view. That's why your response to the other person's feelings matters most of all.

Now, there's a trick to this, and although it might seem manipulative, just remember, if you weren't really listening, you wouldn't be able to do it. So don't feel bad—think of it as using a formula. First rephrase what they've said. Be sure to include the way you perceive they're feeling. Next you need to affirm your motives, to let the other person know where you're coming from, to begin to build trust. In doing so, what you say will have weight, and your suggestions, your advice, and whatever kind of dialogue you're doing will be well received and taken seriously.

When we were shooting the episodes of *Losing It,* the process was intense. I would spend a week tearing through the lives of each family member like a tornado. Then I would leave them on their own to put into practice everything I'd taught them, staying closely in touch by e-mail and phone. Then six weeks later I'd come back to check on their progress. For one young woman, this period when her family was "on their own" became totally stressful, and she stopped responding when I reached out to her. I was deeply concerned that she had gotten off track, and I really needed to get to the bottom of it with her. So I made it as clear as possible that I just wanted to help. Here's roughly how the exchange went:

Me: Rachael, what's been going on with you? I've noticed you're not responding to my e-mails. I'm concerned and confused, and instead of guessing what's going on, I figured I'd just ask you straight out. You can be honest with me. That's what I'm here for.

Rachael: It's not that I'm trying to ignore you. I just feel like I have come to a point where I'm working hard and not seeing the results that you want to see. I'm coming to the point of wanting to give up. I'm so grateful for all your help and support, but sometimes I feel like I'm not doing enough, even though I'm giving it my all. It's discouraging. And I feel like we have to live up to a standard that so far we aren't meeting, which is a slam to the self-esteem.

Watch how I repeat what she said about how I'm making her feel.

Me: I hear you. You are feeling pressured by me, and by the show, to lose weight at a pace you think you aren't capable of and it's making you feel like a failure.

Once Rachael knows I have heard her, that she can trust me to listen to what she's saying, I go on to get to the bottom of this problem.

Me: Do you really want to give up, or are you just feeling afraid? You came to me saying you wanted to change your life. So did you change your mind? Tell me what *you want* for your future.

Rachael: It's hard to put into words the way I feel, but it isn't at all that I don't want this! We all needed and still need your help and encouragement. You know we are a stubborn family, and we want the best results possible. We want to feel good about ourselves; we want to be happier and healthier. I just feel like it takes time, and I feel so much pressure to lose weight for the cameras that I get so discouraged and angry with myself. Please don't get discouraged with us. It's just hard doing all this from a distance and making sure we are all on the same page. I hope this helps you understand where I'm coming from.

Now see how I validate what she has said and give her the power to tell me what I can do to better help her.

Me: I can totally understand how you'd feel overwhelmed by this process. While you're right, I do want you to lose weight for the show, I'm first and foremost here to help you. After all, that's what this show is all about. I'm not discouraged about you at all! I just want to be sure that I'm helping you in the best way possible. It's my understanding that your agenda, my agenda, the agenda of the show, are one and the same. From what you're saying, it sounds like this hasn't changed, so please let me know what I can do to make it easier for you to achieve your goals.

Rachael: I really appreciate your help. I think maybe if you could not ask me how much I weigh unless I bring it up, that would really ease some of the pressure. And if I'm having a bad week, try to understand and not judge me. I'm really grateful for this opportunity, and I'll stay in touch more from now on.

Me: I can do *all* those things! And just know that I don't judge you, not ever. I care about you, and I am here to help you get healthy in whatever capacity best suits you.

Now, let's analyze this exchange for a minute. My first response was to let Rachael know that I heard what she was talking about and understood how she felt. This is not to be confused with my *agreeing* with what she said. People can say things you don't agree with, and you can still understand how they feel. Personally, I didn't think the expectations put on Rachael were unreasonable—I knew she had it in her, and I felt the time and tools that had been given to her were enough. But what I felt was totally irrelevant here. She was feeling overwhelmed and set up to fail, and I had to acknowledge and address those feelings before she'd be able to move on and get healthy. So I summarized the situation and let her know that I understood her feelings of frustration.

But then I went on to do something else, something that's very important for all of us to do in our everyday interactions: I affirmed my motive. I let her know *why* I was having this conversation with her. By being transparent with your motives like this, you can build trust that allows you to forge a more open, productive relationship. In this case, I wanted to build trust so that Rachael could listen to what I had to say, so that I could help her get her life and her health back. Of course this only works if you have positive motives. If your motives are crappy or shady, then you're wasting your time reading this chapter, but I'm going to go with the benefit of the doubt and bet that they're not. You should never be afraid to tell the truth—it's always enough.

I wanted Rachael to lose weight, for her and for the success of the show. I laid my motives out on the table to reinforce her trust, and I then asked her a few key questions about what she needed and how I could help.

LEAD THE WAY

Asking leading questions is the final part of empathic listening. As a listener, your role is to understand. That means you swap your judgment for empathy and your lectures for questions. By asking questions, you show that you are genuinely concerned and want to learn more about what the other person is thinking and feeling. This buys you a huge amount of trust. Look back on the conversations you've had in your own life. Have you ever been on a date with someone who talked the entire time and didn't ask you a single question? Unfortunately, I have. I remember thinking through the whole thing, *Wow, this person is an asshole.* My point here is that if you want to win someone over, then ask them questions about who they are, how they feel, and what they need. These are the things that make all of us feel respected and cared about.

In addition to showing you care, asking questions will help you clarify what the other person needs so you can decide on a course of action that brings about positive resolution. By asking Rachael how I could help her, I ensured our mutual success. She gave me specific directions on what to do and what not to do to facilitate an outcome that was beneficial for both of us.

Mastering leading questions has one other very important benefit. It allows you, in some cases, to bring the other person around to your point of view. It's another slightly manipulative technique, but if done with the best intentions, who cares? And even if you did lead them to it, ultimately they still need to make the choice for themselves, so don't sweat it.

Here's how it works. You can't force change on someone—they have to *choose* it. Although it may seem like I'm doing some forcing on TV, I'm not. It just doesn't work. Think about it: when someone tries to force you to do something, what's your first instinct? Resist, right? The trick is to *help* people arrive at a productive conclusion they can own.

If I had told Rachael what to do, she would have felt bullied, and then she would have resisted. However, by asking her the right questions—"Do you really want to give up, or are you just feeling afraid? You came to me saying you wanted to change your life. So did you change your mind? What do *you want* for your future?"—I helped her realize a better path and was able to bring our agendas into alignment.

This way, there's no power struggle, no fight for control— you're putting the ball in the other person's court and letting them decide. Instead of trying to control Rachael or convince her of my point of view, I led her through a series of pointed questions that laid out the pros and cons of her choices, allowing her eventually to decide for herself that she did want to get healthy and lose weight.

Listening isn't complicated. People want to be heard and feel known—that's at the core of our humanity. To us, listening is love. When we're listened to and understood—not necessarily agreed with, but heard and identified with—we gain the openness and trust required for mutually beneficial collaboration. Of course, this is a two-way street. So next we're going to talk about, well, talking.

SPEAK UP FOR YOURSELF

Your ability to voice your thoughts, feelings, and ideas effectively is just as important as your ability to listen. No man is an island (and no woman either!), and to have a great life, you must be able to collaborate with others.

We have a tendency to idealize individualism in our culture. But remember that island? We don't get anywhere on our own, not truly. Would we have survived as a species over thousands of years without working together? Doubtful. You *have* to work with others if you want to be productive, and the way you speak to others determines whether they're with you or against you.

Whether it's the spouse you fight with constantly, the family members who push food on you, the boss who doesn't like your ideas—whoever it is, other people play a huge role in your success. If you think you can achieve your goal on your own, you're just being foolish. Check your ego at the door—there's no room for it. If you're really in this to make things happen, it's time to swallow your pride.

Getting people on your side peels away so many obstacles to success, and this next section is all about how to do that. Think of this as "how to win friends and influence people"— Jillian style.

The first thing you're going to need is some *cojones*. You're going to have to be brave enough to tell others what you think, how you feel, and what you need. A lot of us take it for granted that our wants and needs are obvious. Well, they're not. People are not mind readers, and most of the time they won't know how to help you unless you tell them. Remember, they're bringing their own experiences and frames of reference to the table just like you are. It could very well be that what they think of as helpful, you find hurtful.

By telling people what you're thinking and feeling, you give them what they need to understand you and work with you. Asking for help and expressing your needs might make you feel vulnerable, awkward, weak, or selfish at first. This is where courage comes into it. But the more you articulate your needs, the more powerful you will become. And let's be honest, if you can't talk about a problem, it can't get resolved.

I'm sure you're thinking, *Oh, I can't do that. It will hurt people's feelings.* Actually, if you express yourself in the right way, you won't hurt anyone's feelings, and I'm hoping you've built up enough self-esteem by this point to let others worry about their own emotional health anyway. Your obligation is to focus on your own.

KEEP AN OPEN MIND

The key to effective communication is keeping an open mind. By keeping an open mind and an open heart, you can focus on the solution, not on the method by which it's reached. At all costs, avoid becoming defensive, assigning blame, or attacking the other person. That is a surefire way to end a conversation before it's begun. You must speak from an empathic place. Remember that the other person has their own feelings and thoughts about things. Be sensitive to that when you are engaging them.

One of the basic techniques for communicating with sensitivity is to use I-statements as opposed to you-statements. This is Communication 101. Framing your conversations with

I-statements lets you discuss your issues without accusing the other person of causing the problem. A you-statement does, well, the opposite.

Here's an easy example:

I was dating a guy a while back who was really close to his buddies. We had gotten to a point where he was hanging out with them more often than not, and although I was a big supporter of his need for male bonding, he never invited me, and I was starting to feel left out and distanced from him. There's no doubt we needed to have a conversation. I could have gone on the offensive and attacked him, like this: "Whenever I do something or go somewhere, I always include you, but when you go out with your friends, you have never once had the common decency to invite me. I've been really cool about it till now, but I'm sick of your acting like a selfish jerk. How would you feel if I were this inconsiderate of your feelings?!" Now, that's how I was feeling on the inside, but communicating my issue that way was going to get me nowhere or probably even make matters worse. He would likely have gotten defensive and argued back, saying something to the effect, "You're such a bitch sometimes. You question why I don't invite you out with us? No wonder I need time alone with my boys." The situation would escalate negatively from there.

If you replace the you-statements with I-statements, however, your chances of reaching a positive outcome increase exponentially. So after I calmed down, this was the path I chose, and this is how the conversation actually went: "Honey, I totally get that you want and need your alone time with your friends. I like time alone with my friends sometimes, too, but lately it feels like it's all the time. And I don't want to intrude or anything, but it would be nice to hang out with you guys once in a while. It makes me feel insecure when you don't invite me, like you don't want me there or you're not proud to show me off, and I feel like I'm becoming less and less a part of your life." And his response was as follows: "Wow, babe, I'm sorry. I had no idea you felt that way. I make plans all the time these days because you've been working so much and

I hate sitting at home by myself waiting for you. Then when you're actually available, I just figure you want to rest because you work all the time and the last thing you'd want to do is go to a hockey game or play poker. I have plans with the guys this Thursday to play pool. Do you want to come?" Crisis averted.

In this scenario, my statement was one of fact. It didn't accuse him of anything, and it thereby left room for him to respond in a more sympathetic way, with no judgment coloring the dialogue. As a result, he acknowledged my feelings, clarified his intention, and suggested a solution. In addition, this conversation showed me how he was feeling about my work schedule, giving me an opportunity to remedy that issue in our relationship as well. Sadly, some things are irreconcilable, and the work thing did eventually break us up, but our solid communication kept our respect and care for each other intact, and we're still close friends to this day.

Now, if the person you are communicating with doesn't respond to an open, nonthreatening dialogue, or if it becomes clear that they have no regard for your feelings even after you have expressed them in a calm, loving way, then this becomes a different issue altogether, and you may want to reevaluate the dynamics of the relationship.

KNOW YOUR AUDIENCE, AND BE WILLING TO COMPROMISE

The personal and professional aspects of your life are going to require slightly different approaches. The communications are going to involve different specifics, but the general principles remain the same. You probably won't utilize I-statements often in your business interactions, or have long talks about feelings, but they still do come into play. In business as in anything, you need to think about where the other person is coming from, so you can try to meet them where they are before expressing your thoughts and ideas. This is the starting point for progress, because this basic principle applies to any conversation. I'm going to give you another example from my professional life, since it's slightly easier for me to analyze and quantify.

After eight seasons of *The Biggest Loser,* I was ready to broaden my TV horizons a bit and embrace new challenges, so I decided to approach NBC to throw around some ideas. I was beyond thrilled to be part of a show as successful as *The Biggest Loser,* and more important, I was humbled and grateful to be able to help change lives.

But I also wanted new challenges. Bottom line, I wanted to expand my platform to a more well-rounded vehicle and get out a broader message of wellness, beyond being part of the *Biggest Loser* team. That's where I was coming from. But as I considered my first move, I also had to think about NBC's needs and perspective. With *Loser,* they had a tiger by the tail. It was their number-one-rated show at the time, and they would want to preserve it. They had also given me my start, and they might think my desire to move on reflected ingratitude. It seems like a tough situation, with two diametrically opposed interests, right? How could we get to a win-win situation?

Well, I sat down with the president of alternative programming at the network and listened carefully to all his concerns and issues. Then I expressed mine. After we appreciated our respective positions, we started looking for a solution that would expand my platform without taking me away from *Biggest Loser.* And that's how *Losing It with Jillian* was born—compromise! I agreed to stay on in exchange for my own spin-off show, where I got to really help people in all aspects of their lives. With both parties gaining, this solution was the very definition of win-win.

Now, this conversation could have gone *very* differently. I could have gone in angry and screaming about all the things I felt were unjust over my six-year run on *Loser.* And the president could have come to the table power-tripping and played the "We made you, we'll break you" card. I guarantee you, a small part of each of us *totally* felt like doing that. As intelligent business people, however, we also understood that an interaction fueled by those kinds of crappy, ego-based attitudes would get us nowhere.

Instead, he spoke his mind in a way that took my position into account, and vice versa—and that left us open to a host of possible solutions.

The big lesson here is that you can always find a way to engage other people that makes them part of the solution, not part of the problem. When you speak in a way that's not only true to your own dreams but also considerate of other people's, you enlist people instead of turning them off. And before you know it, your dream grows and takes on forms you never could have imagined.

Above all, cultivate mutual respect, the foundation for any successful interaction. Give respect freely to others, and command it for yourself. Approach a conversation this way, and it's unlikely that anyone will feel undervalued, attacked, taken advantage of, or demeaned. Instead, you're likely to come to a result that is good for everyone involved. There is almost always a way, no matter how difficult the person or the exchange.

One last tip for becoming a highly effective communicator: rehearse what you want to say beforehand. As in, out loud. Say it to the cat, say it to the mirror, but *say it*. No matter how much you've thought something through, putting it into words is going to be different. The more you've run through the major points you want to make, the basic order of what you're going to say, the more confident you'll be when it comes time to engage the other person or people.

If you're going into a really big conversation—asking for a promotion, or confronting a loved one about something sensitive—you may even want to role-play with a good friend. This will allow you to walk through various scenarios so that when you're in the moment, you won't be shaken or impulsive with your responses. That will help you maintain control of the conversation and keep it moving forward in a positive and productive direction.

Remember, communicating well is something you can and must work at. Practice it in every interaction you have, whether it's at the supermarket checkout or meeting your boyfriend's parents for the first time.

The objective is always to open a constructive dialogue that is calm, thoughtful, considerate, and clear. If you have fears and concerns, put them on the table for discussion without judgment or accusation. Give others the opening to jump in and become a source of support rather than sabotage.

Not everyone is going to respond positively to open dialogue. If problems arise, you need to accept that you've tried, realize that the unresolved issue speaks to their limitations, not yours, and move on. But before doing that, make sure you've done what you can to negotiate the situation—which is up next.

EXTRA CREDIT: NEGOTIATION

Like it or not, most of our interactions come down to a negotiation of some kind. And although it sounds cold and clinical, negotiating is simply arriving at an agreement that allows forward momentum. As the old Rolling Stones song says, "You can't always get what you want, but if you try sometimes, well you just might find you get what you need."

Whether you're fighting with your spouse about where to have the family vacation, buying a home, or hashing out a multimillion-dollar business deal, you need the same tactics and skills. This isn't to say we're all mercenaries out fighting for our own self-serving agendas. It's not about world domination or subjugating people to your will. Win-win is the name of the game, and the goal is for both parties to feel positive about the negotiation once it's over. This helps good, positive relationships to continue after the fact and allows for a level of cooperation that will take you to new heights.

Sometimes a win-lose negotiation is unavoidable, but you should really resort to it only if you don't have to maintain an ongoing relationship with the other party. Having come up short, they may not want to deal with you in the future. Consider that if you are going to want anything from them, or if they have yet to fulfill part of a deal in which you have "won," they may be uncooperative.

In my own experience, whenever I have felt duped or cheated,

I have done the bare minimum to fulfill whatever agreement was in place and then had no further dealings with that party. For my second set of exercise DVDs, my old team negotiated what I later discovered was a very bad deal for me. The DVDs were massive best sellers, but because of loopholes in my contract, I barely saw a dime. I had three DVDs left to shoot with this company before my deal was up. I put my best foot forward, because I wanted people to get their money's worth when they bought the DVDs, but when that deal was up, I didn't renegotiate to extend my contract.

By that point my DVDs made up 50 percent of the top-ten-selling fitness titles on the market, and my decision limited the company's future growth in the category. The DVD market share of the company I subsequently signed with grew to first place. *And now I'm auditing the first company for unpaid royalties.*

The moral of the story?

Don't ever think you're pulling one over on someone when you stiff them, and don't be greedy, because karma is a bitch and it will always come back to you in the end. It's best not to sour any relationship, if you can possibly avoid it.

To master negotiation, you'll need to hone both your speaking and your listening skills. And as with everything, preparation is key.

WORKING IT OUT

CONSIDER YOUR GOALS AND THE GOALS OF THE OTHER PERSON

What do you want to get out of this situation? What do you think the other person wants out of it?

THINK ABOUT WHAT YOU ARE WILLING TO GIVE UP

Compromise is pretty much always necessary. Prioritize the things you want to achieve, and think about what you are willing to sacrifice to arrive at a resolution.

HAVE AT LEAST ONE PLAN B

If you can't reach a win-win agreement, what other options do you have? What are the ramifications of each? If things don't go the way you hope, you don't want to be thrown off. Have a backup plan, so you'll be coming from a place of strength rather than weakness.

LEARN FROM THE PAST

Is there a history you can learn from, or precedents you can look to for guidance? Have you or the other party had similar negotiations in the past? If so, what was the outcome, and why? By understanding previous conversations, you can circumvent established pitfalls and avoid making the same mistake twice.

The holidays are usually the only times I ever get to travel for pleasure. My mother demands a family Christmas come hell or high water. She will make concessions on Thanksgiving or New Year's if I have to work or I'm traveling, but I have learned my lesson, and Christmas is sacred. Don't mess with that. All else is fair game.

MAKE A LIST OF ALL POSSIBLE SOLUTIONS

Based on all these considerations, what possible compromises could be reached to arrive at a win-win finish line? Let's take the family vacation discussion again. You want to spend your vacation with your ailing grandmother. Your husband wants to take a family ski trip. Possible solutions include taking the grandmother with you on the ski trip, splitting the vacation time between the two options, or taking the ski trip but also setting aside some time before or after the holiday to spend visiting Grandma.

QUIZ
Are You a Master or a Disaster at Communicating?

THEN THINK ON THIS

Above all else, you must always go into an exchange, whether it's with a friend, a loved one, a colleague, or a superior, with the intention of keeping your heart and mind flexible, open to new alternatives, opinions, and possibilities.

Remember not to get caught in power struggles caused by ego.

Strong disagreements and failed negotiations can create all kinds of problems and hold you back in so many ways. What's more, over time they can poison even the warmest, most loving relationships. Practice and use what you've learned here to create happiness and harmony in your life and in the lives of those around you. You'll be amazed at how honing these communication skills will help you in all things great and small.

CHAPTER THIRTEEN

STRENGTHEN WILLPOWER AND TAME EMOTIONS

Being irrational and acting impulsively are big roadblocks to mastering communication skills. Although willpower and emotion regulation are two separate things, they go hand in hand. Irrational feelings often make us impulsive, and if we can control impulsivity, we buy ourselves time to reason and create proactive, empowering solutions. Never forget, one moment of unchecked impulsivity can destroy months or even years of hard work, so it's well worth practicing keeping it together. By better managing your emotions, especially the negative ones, you can significantly increase your chances of success in every part of your life.

In my own struggles with willpower and impulsivity, I've come to realize that will is a skill, not a myth or a genetic trait. Anyone can develop it at any point. And that is the focus of this chapter.

Remember, no matter how strong your self-control may become, like the muscle that gets fatigued, it can get overworked and burn out on you. Notice that you're likely to lose your temper at the end of a long, grueling day. Notice how you kick ass on your diet all day long, and then in the middle of the night when you are exhausted and your mind is spinning in stress circles, you find yourself peering into the fridge, looking for trouble. I guarantee you, it's always that *last* straw that breaks the camel's back. This is exactly why we discussed controlling your environment (in Chapter 11) and eliminating sources of sabotage (in Chapter 5). The goal of all that was to get you to hold your willpower in reserve for moments when temptation *can't* be avoided.

Ideally, we *avoid* negativity and temptation, but sometimes they just can't be avoided. So you need to learn how to strengthen your willpower and to manage your emotions for those particularly trying times. You can avoid trouble for only so long. And when it comes up, you'd better be ready for it.

USING YOUR BRAIN: THE TECHNIQUE

What proactive steps can you take to keep your impulses under control? Simple: change *where* you think. Literally. Certain parts of your brain are prone to instinct and impulsivity, while other parts are prone to reason and contemplation.

The amygdala is the part of your brain that's wired for quick emotional processing based on your body's immediate needs. Its job is to make the quick fight-or-flight decisions required in survival situations. It tells you to run when you see a bear in the woods, then actually gives you the boost to take off running.

On the opposite end of the spectrum is your frontal lobe, dedicated to reasoning and contemplation. It is emotion-neutral, and its main purpose is problem-solving. This part of our brains allowed the cavemen to develop the tools that eventually moved them out of the cave and toward a more agrarian lifestyle.

Now, here's where we often go wrong: we choose the wrong part of our brain for the wrong task. Suppose your boss tells you at five P.M. that he wants your report on his desk by morning. You get pissed at your boss, tell him to shove it, and get fired. Thank you, amygdala. Your frontal lobe would have taken a breath, gone into your boss's office after things had cooled down, reasoned with him, and come up with a viable solution. Maybe you'd have worked out an extension till midafternoon, or possibly you'd have gotten another coworker with you on the job.

On the same note, suppose you saw a bear in the woods and stopped to think about it. Chances are you'd become bear dinner before ever arriving at a conclusion about what to do. So you see, both parts of the brain have a specific and necessary purpose. Success is a matter of knowing what part of your brain to use when, and, most important, how to control which part of the brain you are using.

I'm going to make this really easy: in most situations, you'll want to use your frontal lobe. Unless you are in *immediate life-threatening danger,* you should always be using the more rational, contemplative part of your brain to process and react to the world around you. The amygdala is often the first to respond, just on instinct, but you can reroute the action to the more reasoncentric frontal lobe.

Believe it or not, you achieve this by arguing with yourself and your emotions.

Let me explain. Active strategies such as classifying, debating, deliberating, and delaying get the frontal lobe engaged, thus changing the center of activity in the brain from impulse central to rational city, which is where we want to be.

Here's the step-by-step:

1. You're overwhelmed with emotion, and your first instinct is to lash out and do something rash and dramatic. The second you feel this way, STOP! Literally stop everything you are doing and stand still in your tracks.

2. Take five deep breaths. Deep breathing helps release stress and calms the mind. Yogis say that you can't hold any tension in the body when you're moving through a breath.

3. Now, carefully contemplate and ruminate on the possible results of your decisions and actions, *before* you actually commit to

them. This will allow you to move from a "go" state, where you are impulsive and reactionary, to a "know" state, where you are able to take a long-term view and act in your ultimate best interest.

All of life's answers and solutions may not come to you in one enlightened moment of meditative contemplation. But you can be certain that if you take that enlightened moment, you won't end up doing massive damage by making a rash decision, like telling your boss where to stick it or bingeing on Flamin' Hot Cheetos at one A.M.

BLESSINGS IN DISGUISE

Effective emotion regulation is vital for healthy life management and adaptation to the changes and curveballs that *will* come our way. I can promise you, shit is going to happen. Hence the bumper sticker. No matter what you do to try to take control, you can't control Life. What you *can* control is how you handle it.

In fact, many of life's hardships and struggles happen for good reasons. The key is to find that often-elusive silver lining. And that, in a nutshell, is the best way to manage negative emotions. This silver lining approach to life actually has a fancy scientific title. It's called cognitive reappraisal. It's a coping strategy that involves monitoring and evaluating negative thoughts and replacing them with more positive thoughts and images. When we reframe painful or frightening events with a positive meaning, we decrease their negative emotional impact (stress, depression, sadness, etc.). According to this theory, it is how we think about, or "appraise," the meaning of our experiences that gives rise to our emotions, good and bad.

This may sound very similar to logotherapy, which we discussed in Chapter 7. That's because it is. But there's one major difference. In logotherapy, you create a purpose for a catastrophic event as a means of grief management. There's no silver lining. In cognitive reappraisal, you emphasize the positive aspects of an event and deemphasize the negative. This much broader technique applies to nearly everything in your life, because nearly everything has pros and cons. In other words, you're looking for the blessing in disguise.

This business parable that someone once shared with me perfectly illustrates my point. Two men enter into business together as partners in a shoe company. One of the men goes to Africa to expand his horizons. Upon arriving there, he realizes that none of the natives wear shoes. He is utterly beside himself, and sends word to his partner: "Just arrived in Africa. No one wears shoes here." The next day, as he is packing his bags to head home, he receives a telegram from his partner: "That's WONDERFUL! An entire country of people who need our product, and we are the first on the scene. We are going to be rich!"

Now, you could have looked at this situation from either perspective. But which one is going to get you where you want to go? You know it before I write it here. I guarantee that if you always look for the positive, things will work out more positively.

Here's another example, one that I had a hand in. On *Losing It* I worked with a dad named Mark Vivio who had fallen upon very hard times, physically, financially, and emotionally. It all started when a bridge he had built to connect two parts of his property collapsed. When the bridge went down, Mark went down with it, and subsequently he tore the ACL in his knee. His family rushed him to the hospital, where they discovered in the course of prepping him for knee surgery that he had a life-threatening heart condition that would require multiple surgeries. By the time I met him, he'd had thirteen. The surgeries left Mark unable to work, which forced him to close his roofing business.

All of this in one year!

Mark was devastated when I met him. The collapse of the bridge, which he referred to as "the downfall of man," seemed symbolic of his life falling into irreversible ruin. His depression was debilitating to him and was tearing his family apart.

This is where cognitive reappraisal comes in handy. How

can we frame this series of events so as to take something positive from it? Well, if Mark hadn't built the bridge, it wouldn't have collapsed. If it hadn't collapsed, he wouldn't have injured his knee. But if he'd never injured his knee, he would never have discovered his heart condition and most likely would have died within the year.

Does undergoing multiple heart surgeries suck? Totally. Does being incapacitated suck? Completely. Does losing your business and not being able to support your family suck eggs? Unbelievably. It's fair to say, however, that had the bridge never collapsed, Mark probably wouldn't be alive. So no matter how awful his woes, widowing your wife and leaving four kids without a dad is way worse.

Ultimately, Mark was able to realize that he had been given a second chance. And that motivated him to reclaim his health, which will keep him around for years to come. Although Mark's roofing business had supported everyone, he never really loved the work. Finding himself at a crossroads, he reinvented himself to pursue a career as a state trooper, something he'd wanted since being a kid.

He could have let all those sad events crush him. He could have thrown in the towel and lived out the rest of his life in quiet desperation. Instead he brought meaning to these hardships and allowed them to catapult his life to new levels of happiness and health.

CRUSHED OR AWAKENED?

On *Losing It,* I met a woman whose husband of thirty years had cheated on her, and they had divorced. She was lost, confused, mortified. In truth, she had outgrown the marriage years before his infidelity. They weren't in love anymore, but they cared for each other and stayed together for the sake of the kids and because "that's just what you do."

When I met her, about two years after they finally divorced, she was still reeling from the upheaval. I began teaching her the techniques of cognitive reappraisal by getting her to think of positive possibilities to her newfound "freedom." How could she use this painful event to help catalyze a new beginning for herself?

What about the marriage had left her unfulfilled? I asked. Why did she settle in her personal relationships? What kind of person did she want to spend the rest of her life with? How good would it feel to be in love again? How often in the marriage had she put everyone else's needs in front of her own? How could she take this opportunity to start prioritizing her own well-being? Well, she did renew her lease on life, and now she's happily dating the man of her dreams. Had her husband never cheated on her, she never would have found a man who brings her true happiness.

One last one . . .

A friend of mind got laid off from his office job. He was devastated. He panicked. How would he make money? Who was he without his job? What would people think? But eventually, when he calmed down and thought things through, he realized he'd hated his job, and maybe this was the universe's way of telling him not to waste any more time just surviving when he could be thriving. He'd always loved sports and wanted to work in fitness. He applied for student loans, got a part-time job as a trainer, and went back to school to become a physical therapist. And now he has a very successful and fulfilling practice in Manhattan.

We will all face challenging circumstances from time to time. But the way we think about and process these situations can increase or decrease the suffering we experience and can determine what we make of the hand that's dealt us.

Always look for the deeper meaning. I promise you that even the most trying hardships hold beautiful lessons, and we can always be better and stronger in the long run, no matter what may knock us down momentarily. The key is to be brave enough to stay open, look for the lesson, and do the hard work of self-exploration that leads from breakdown to breakthrough.

Once you have reassigned the emotional associations of your life's struggles from negative to positive, it's time to take the next step, putting it all together and creating the life you want. In this next chapter you'll learn how to move from awareness to transformation. Now that you've stopped your self-sabotaging behaviors, you need to follow up with strong decisions and productive actions. Let's get to it.

CHAPTER FOURTEEN

MAKE IT HAPPEN

The Art of Conscious Choice-Making

Okay, this is the last chapter in our travels together and perhaps the most powerful action step. It will require you to utilize all the previous lessons this book has taught you synergistically, to piece the passages of music together and play the entire song. You'll need the passion that you cultivated in Step One because your dream will be driving your choices. Then you'll need to muster the awareness and self-esteem that you established in Step Two in order to bring consciousness and faith to the process. And finally you'll need the same methodical discipline that you have been practicing throughout Step Three.

We've talked a lot about specific ways you can move toward the life of your dreams. But ultimately your future is determined by your choices—it's that simple. Creating your own future is within your capability and grasp. You are already doing it, for better or worse.

We are all, right now, living the life we are choosing.

So if you're unhappy, it's because you're making the wrong choices.

I'm not talking about one momentous *choice* that either catapults you to success or plunges you into failure, ruin, and regret. I'm talking about *choices*—plural. The ones you make daily, hourly, from moment to moment, the ones that you haven't mindfully planned out. You might think that once you've organized your daily routine and environment, life will run smoothly and efficiently along the tracks, just as you want it to. But there's more to it.

We make hundreds if not thousands of choices every day that dramatically affect the direction and expression of our lives, from whether to brush our teeth in the morning, to what health insurance to buy, to how we speak to our coworkers, friends, and family, to what we eat for dinner. More often than not, the unconscious decisions end up wreaking havoc.

A bad choice that's made consciously can be acknowledged, learned from, and then tweaked to bring a better future outcome. But a bad choice that's made unconsciously goes unfixed and often leaves you feeling defeated, powerless, and victimized. Bad choices are insidious because once you become a victim in your own mind, you give up responsibility and control. But you need that control to make your dreams a reality.

A contestant on *The Biggest Loser* went through all the right motions to get on the show. Once on the show, he was totally focused on hitting his targeted weekly weight-loss goals so he could stay on campus and continue getting healthy. I meticulously planned out his goal pyramid with him so he would know exactly what actions to take to make his dream of weight loss, health, and possibly winning the contest a reality.

For several weeks he was doing all his tasks, from cooking healthy food to counting calories to getting his sleep to taking his vitamins. He was the perfect contestant. Then without warning he developed a massive toothache. The next thing he knew, he was in the dentist's chair for most of a week getting oral surgery on two root canals. So he missed tons of workout time. He was put on antibiotics, which is not great for the metabolism. He could eat only mushy foods and wasn't able to stay on the diet I had recommended. Sure enough, at that week's weigh-in, he fell below the line and got sent home.

Back at home, my determined former contestant was in tears with me on the phone. "Why did this happen to me? Every time I start something in my life, it falls apart. No matter what I do, I'm cursed with bad luck." On and on. What he failed to see was the enormous part that *his own choices* played in his current situation. When I said on the previous page that simple daily decisions like whether to brush your teeth can affect your life, I wasn't kidding! If my contestant had taken better care of his teeth, flossed, invested twenty-two dollars in a power tooth-brush, and eaten slightly better, his chances of having all those dental issues would have been drastically reduced, and he might not have sabotaged his *Biggest Loser* journey. He might actually have gone on to win the whole show and been not only healthy but $250,000 richer.

Every action we do, every choice we make, has a direct and dramatic impact on our lives. Unfortunately, many of these seemingly little decisions are made unconsciously, and that is where the sabotage takes root. My contestant wasn't thinking about the future when he was brushing his teeth. He was probably half asleep, going through the motions, and rushing to get out the door for work, or rushing to get to bed. Years later, he paid the price for his absence of thought.

THE BEST PATH ISN'T ALWAYS THE EASIEST ONE

I'm going to give you one more example to really drive my point home. You go through life eating processed fast food because you reckon it's easy and cheap, and because maybe it's what you ate growing up. We don't really think about the longer term when we're making the grab for fast food. At that moment, we're usually thinking about something else, some other matter in our busy lives. Fast food is convenient and comfortable, and the last thing we need is more work. Or so we think.

But one day you're diagnosed with heart disease, or cancer, or diabetes, or some other horrible illness brought on by poor nutrition and lifestyle choices. The medical bills practically and perhaps literally bankrupt you and your family. You start to feel victimized, persecuted. *Why did this have to happen to me?* You throw a pity party, invite yourself, and never leave.

Sure, this is a heavy scenario to contemplate, but it's not out of the realm of possibility, far from it. In fact, heart disease is the number-one killer in this country. Every twenty seconds an American has a heart attack. Every thirty-four seconds one of us dies from heart disease. The cancer statistics are equally scary. Sadly, this is more likely your reality than not, and if you would just wake the hell up, chances are you could cut down your risk of all this misery significantly.

If you had thought through your choices when you were making them, your situation would most likely be very different. What if you had swapped out the fries for a side salad? What if you had asked for your food grilled instead of accepting it sautéed and fried? What if you had invested that extra twenty dollars a week in healthy groceries instead of gossip rags, crappuccinos, or whatever? What if you had taken the time to bring healthy food from home to work instead of hitting the drive-through or buying the nearest processed food at hand? What if you had taken the time to exercise thirty minutes a day instead of watching *The Backstabbing Housewives from God Knows Where*? I'll tell you what! There's a 99 percent chance you wouldn't have gotten sick or have bankrupted yourself treating a preventable disease. You'd probably be happy, healthy, and looking at many more quality years to come.

My goal isn't to make you obsess over everything you do, or to trap you in a game of "what if." It's not to make you feel bad about the choices you've made in the past, or the choices you are currently making. The point, again, is to be present. The fact is you're here, now, ready to start bringing more awareness to the things you do every day. We want to bring mindfulness into your daily routine so you're firing on all cylinders and exponentially enhancing your chances of success and a high-quality life.

You are in control!

Life doesn't happen to you—you happen to it.

You can't foresee everything that might come at you, and you can't micromanage your life to setback-free perfection. But you *can* control your choices, actions, and reactions. And that's all it takes to build happiness, no matter what life serves up.

By now you have realized the tremendous importance of the power of choice, a recurring theme in this book. Here we will practice exercises for *how* to make powerful, positive choices to effect powerful, positive change.

Start by becoming aware of your unconscious decisions. Then you can bring your best intentions to those choices, to help direct your life toward your desired result. Remember, mindlessness is often the root of self-destruction. We go numb, we check out, and we're unable to think through our actions and choices. Before long, we're reacting unconsciously and/or subconsciously to life in ways that blow us way off course.

WORKING IT OUT

Here are a few exercises to help you take control of your destiny!

PRESS THE PAUSE BUTTON

Stop and question what you're doing before you take action. This tactic works well for managing impulsivity and building willpower, but it also brings a basic thoughtfulness into your daily life, allowing you control over your fate. Take a brief pause before every action, and ask yourself the following questions:

What am I doing in this moment?

Is there a choice to be made here? If so, what choice am I making?

Will this choice bring me happiness and bring me closer to my
long-term goals?

These questions are all you need to decipher whether something
will hurt you or help you in the long run. Keep them in the fore-
front of your mind, and they can serve as your internal compass,
your GPS, helping you stay on track throughout your day, week,
month, year, and life.

A contestant on season ten named Jesse was feeling lost and
out of control, so one day we sat down, and I asked him to identify
a few key long-term goals. One of them, it turns out, was wearing
a tie. He said he couldn't wear a tie because he was "too big and
didn't have a neck." Not being able to wear a tie hindered him on
job interviews, he thought, and kept him from dressing nicely at
events or on dates. Long story short, wearing a tie was the symbol
of everything he felt was out of reach because of his weight. So I
told him that before he made every choice that day, he should ask
himself whether the end result of that choice would get him closer
to wearing a tie. If the answer was yes, then go for it. If no, then
make a different choice.

That morning Jesse skipped the almond butter toast for breakfast and opted for an egg-white veggie omelet instead. Then he
decided to give up his chance to sleep an extra hour in order to
squeeze in some cardio before his day began. He wrapped his ankle
before his second afternoon hike to make sure he didn't injure
himself on the trail. That night he skipped the game-playing gossip and shenanigans that the contestants do behind closed doors
before bed, and he opted for an early night's sleep to help speed
his metabolism. Having his goal in his mind at all times brought
focus to his actions, even to the small ones that we often don't
think about.

Use this strategy to map out a clear course of action that puts
you back in the game instead of walking on the sidelines. Oh, and
by the way, Jesse was beaming from ear to ear at the *Biggest Loser*
finale in his dapper bow tie.

TILT AT WINDMILLS

See every choice and action as a moral quest or a personally defining moment. Don't brush off the smaller moments in life, as they add up to our ultimate happiness. Give every decision and action the respect it deserves. This doesn't have to be overwhelmingly time-consuming. Many choices you make repeat themselves throughout your life, like brushing your teeth. Once you think a choice through, you don't have to contemplate it each time. (That said, it's important not to rush through brushing! Did you know that using the proper toothbrush and toothpaste, and spending the proper amount of time brushing, can help prevent heart disease and save you thousands in dental work?)

Again, this choice is so simple, but it can make a big difference.

LISTEN TO YOUR GUT

Literally. Often when you are about to make a bad choice, your body lets you know. Think of it as a built-in survival mechanism that warns you away from crappy choices that lead you down a crappy path. There's also some actual science behind this theory. Your gut intuition is basically the act of tapping into your subconscious mind, the place where you store information that you don't necessarily remember at a conscious level. So your gut instinct will register as a physical "feeling" that you can't quite articulate. But just because you can't articulate it doesn't mean it's not valid. If contemplating a possible option or decision makes you feel uneasy in your heart, pressure on your chest, or sick in your gut, don't do it! Or take a step back and revisit the "press pause" advice.

Conversely, if a feeling of calm comes over you, it could be a sign to move forward or explore the choice in more depth. I'm telling you, there is something to this listen-to-your-gut stuff. It works. Respect it!

Conscious choice-making is an empowering art form that takes time to perfect, but it's an integral tool in controlling your destiny, so be patient and stick with it. Practice the exercises, and I guarantee you your life will improve dramatically.

Remember, don't let life happen to you. Make it happen for you.

You now have all the tools you need to start building the life you want and deserve. It's time to throw down, lay it on the line, and "go for it." But there's just one more thing I want to leave you with . . .

WHEN TO LET GO, HOW TO STAY OPEN

We're at the end, or the beginning, depending on your point of view, and this is my final message, my parting shot. Let's say you follow every bit of advice I have doled out in this book to the letter. You give the steps a reasonable amount of time to sink in, take hold, and become real in your life. But one of your dreams still hasn't come true. What then?

Now, you know me, I'm not one to ever say die. The very mention of the word *quit* makes my stomach turn. That said, there *is* a time to let go. There's a *huge* difference between quitting in the sense of surrendering and letting go but staying open to alternative outcomes. To quit means to stop trying, and to surrender means you accept defeat. "Screw that!"

This said, there are some things you'll never be able to change. The solutions to your problems don't lie in defying the laws of nature, but in accepting them, and changing your actions to adapt accordingly.

Patience, diligence, and resilience are eventually rewarded with success. We are meant to chase our dreams with zeal and fervor until we catch them. We're supposed to exhaust every option, try every avenue, in pursuit of the life we want. In fact, a huge part of success is a simple matter of showing up and refusing to give up. There may well come a point, however, when you have done all that you can, yet success continues to elude you.

At this point it becomes a matter not of quitting but of letting go and staying open to an outcome you may not yet have in mind. This is about trusting yourself, and trusting in the universe/God/fate/whatever you believe in that's bigger than you, to do right by you and your intentions.

This principle holds true for every level of the journey, including the point at which you have done everything possible but still come up short. To continue pursuing the same goal in the same way unsuccessfully is madness, right? We want to *avoid* making the same mistakes, and concurrently make sure that we are staying open to "divine intervention," whatever that might mean to you personally.

When you trust in yourself and the universe, you open your life to infinite possibilities that you may never have thought of. And the more open you are, the greater your ability to receive happiness.

Life is constantly changing. That's the definition of life, isn't it? With every breath is change. And as you evolve, your commitments, beliefs, and energies will need to continually be refocused and redefined. So will your goals. Be fluid and open. Nothing is stable, nothing is permanent. And yes, for my last cliché, pretty much the only thing that's constant is change and perhaps conflict. But that keeps life interesting and keeps us mixing it up creatively. Occasionally the things that we think are best for us may not be our destiny, and when we stay open, our true path reveals itself. Remember that every seed of good intention you plant will yield fruit. Maybe not at the time or in the form you expect, but it will manifest. Think back to the story I told you about how I ended up on *The Biggest Loser*. I had to fail in one career to find my destiny in another. Stories like that happen every day. Oprah started out wanting to be a news anchor, and Ellen DeGeneres a stand-up comedienne/sitcom star. Massive failures derailed those plans and set them both on a different path, one where their energies and efforts could bring the result that fate intended: huge success.

The reason I'm leaving you with this thought is that sometimes, when we pursue a dream and it doesn't work out, we perceive it as failure. We perceive *ourselves* as failures. But I want you to always remember that failure is just an opportunity for learning, and in many cases a stepping-stone on an unexpected path of success that you can see only in hindsight. From it you can learn a necessary lesson, or create a building block to step forward onto your trajectory toward triumph, whatever that particular triumph may be.

Be brave and be patient. Have faith in yourself; trust in the significance and purpose of your life and your passion. You *are* strong enough to weather this journey. No matter what, keep looking, keep listening, keep learning. Stay open. At every moment, your destiny *is* awaiting you.

INDEX

H

I

J

K

You've seen her change lives and guide others to achieve their maximum health and wellness for years — let her help you.